Studies in
Acts

WILLIAM J. FALLIS

BROADMAN PRESS

NASHVILLE, TENNESSEE

Printed in the United States of America
100AT493

FOREWORD

THE SUNDAY SCHOOL TRAINING COURSE

The Sunday School Training Course prepared by the Sunday School Department of the Baptist Sunday School Board is one of the major means of promoting Sunday school work. Its influence is limited only by its use.

The six sections of the course include studies in Bible, doctrines, evangelism, Sunday school leadership and administration, teaching, age group studies, and special studies. The range of the course is broad, for the field of Sunday school work is broad and requires comprehensive and specific training. Sixteen books are required for the completion of each Diploma.

The study of the Training Course is not to be limited to the present Sunday school workers. Most churches need twice as many workers as are now enlisted. This need can be supplied by training additional workers now. Members of the Young People's and Adult classes and older Intermediates should be led to study these books, for thereby will their service be assured. Parents will find help as they study what the Sunday school is trying to do.

Write to your state Sunday school secretary or to the Sunday School Department, Baptist Sunday School Board, Nashville 3, Tennessee, for a list of the books and other information.

SPECIAL NOTE TO INSTRUCTORS:

During your teaching of this book will you check with the Sunday school superintendent and see if an accurate record of training for the workers is kept. If not, please urge him to set up such a file with an associate superintendent of training in charge. File cards for this purpose will be supplied free of charge upon request. For further information, write to the Sunday School Department, Baptist Sunday School Board, Nashville, 3, Tennessee.

J. N. BARNETTE

Secretary, Sunday School Department
Baptist Sunday School Board

CONTENTS

REQUIREMENTS FOR CREDIT ON THIS BOOK

I. For Teachers of the Course

1. Ten class periods of forty-five minutes each are needed for the completion of a book.

2. Teachers of classes are given, without special examination, the same award as is provided for the classes which they teach.

II. For Members of the Class

1. The student must be fifteen years of age or older.

2. The student must attend at least six forty-five minute class periods. Students who attend as many as five class periods will be granted an award only when the following plan is used:

Take the usual written examination on the chapters studied and discussed in class.

Study the remaining chapters of the book in accordance with the requirements of the individual method and hand the paper to the class teacher.

3. The student must take a written examination, making a minimum grade of 70 per cent.

4. The student must certify that the textbook has been read. (In rare cases where students may find it impracticable to read the book before the completion of the classwork, the teacher may accept a promise to read the book carefully within the next two weeks.)

III. For Individual Study

Those who for any reason wish to study the book without the guidance of a teacher will use one of the follwing methods:

1. Write answers to the questions printed in the book, or

2. Write a development of the chapter outlines.

If the first method is used, the student will study the book and then with the open book write answers to the printed questions.

If the second method is used, the student will study the book and then with the open book write a development of the chapter outlines.

Students may find profit in studying the text together, but individual papers are required. Carbon copies or duplicates in any form cannot be accepted.

All written work done by such students should be sent to the State Sunday School Secretary.

INTRODUCTION

No book in the Bible tells a more thrilling story than the book of Acts. From the wondrous miracle at Pentecost to the awesome storm at sea, it recounts dramatic adventures of Spirit-led men. In its twenty-eight chapters we find the basic outline of the New Testament pattern for twentieth-century churches—in faith, in fellowship, in evangelism, in stewardship, in living and dying for the Lord. Acts is the unique historical link between the earthly ministry of Jesus Christ and all that God has accomplished in men through him in succeeding centuries. It is just the book to be used by the Spirit in bolstering our faith, opening our eyes to world need, and spurring us on as witnesses of the risen Christ.

AUTHOR

Luke is generally credited with having written both the book of Acts and the Gospel that bears his name. He seems to have been a Gentile, probably a Greek. Paul called him "Luke the beloved physician" (Col. 4:14), and as a member of that profession he was doubtless well educated and appreciative of culture. We do not know when Luke became a Christian, but Acts 16:10 suggests that he was not a new convert when Paul had his vision at Troas. He was not merely a traveling companion and physician to the great missionary; Paul listed him with "my fellow workers" (Philem. 24). Another aspect of Luke's character and career is revealed in Paul's last reference to him: "only Luke is with me" (2 Tim. 4:11). Humanly speaking, except for Paul we might never have heard of Luke. On the other hand, what would we know of Paul had it not been for Luke the physician and historian?

Date

Once we have settled on Luke as the author of Acts, the problem of its date is simplified considerably. Certainly it could not have been completed before Paul's arrival in Rome, about A.D. 60. The book was not finished for two years after Paul's arrival in Rome (Acts 28:30). In other words, the book must have been written by A.D. 63.

Purpose

Luke's purpose in writing Acts is not perfectly clear. Of course when we read the first verse in the light of Luke 1:1-4, we see Acts as a sequel to the Gospel, and the purpose of the Gospel may be projected into the book of Acts. The sequel would tell how Jesus' followers lived and witnessed under the leadership of the Spirit. Whether Luke had any more specific purpose in mind, we cannot say. Some scholars have argued that Luke wrote the book with the hope that it might be useful to Paul during his trial. The book is not a complete history of early Christianity, nor is it a complete biography of Paul. Therefore, even though it was not entitled "the Gospel of the Holy Spirit," Luke's purpose does seem to have been to recount the varied and powerful influence of the Spirit on men in the early spread of Christianity. His purpose was thus shaped by divine inspiration.

Chronology

Since Luke did not use our modern calendar, nor was he always specific in his references to time, we cannot positively fix the chronology of the book. According to the research of Dr. A. T. Robertson, these four dates stand out as certain: (1) ascension and Pentecost, A.D. 29; (2) Herod's death, A.D. 44; (3) Paul's visit to Corinth, A.D. 50-52; (4) Paul's imprisonment in Caesarea, A.D. 57-59.

How This Book Can Help

This book was written to help you in your study of Acts; it cannot be fully understood unless the reader keeps his New Testament open and follows Luke's story, paragraph by paragraph. Chapter titles were chosen as characteristic of the biblical content treated in the various chapters; some of them might be applied to other sections or to the whole book of Acts. But these chapter titles suggest a standard for measuring a New Testament church in any era. As you study, measure your own church by the standards set in the first-century churches.

Acknowledgements

Four books especially have given me insight and inspiration, and I have quoted from them frequently, indicating the source in parentheses:

(1) Carver, William Owen. *The Acts of the Apostles*. Nashville: Broadman Press, 1916. (2) Hackett, Horatio B. "An American Commentary of the New Testament," *Acts*. Philadelphia: American Baptist Publication Society, 1882. (3) Robertson, A. T. "Word Pictures in the New Testament," *Acts*. Nashville: Baptist Sunday School Board, 1930. (4) Smith, Miles W. *On Whom the Spirit Came*. Philadelphia: Judson Press, 1948.

Sources of Scripture quotations, other than the King James Version (KJV), have been indicated as: ASV, American Standard Version, and RSV, Revised Standard Version; both of which are copyrighted by the International Council of Religious Education. All copyrighted material has been used by permission.

EMPOWERED BY THE SPIRIT

Acts 1:1 to 2:41

I. *The Promise of the Spirit* (1:1-11)

    1. From the Gospel to Acts (1-3)
    2. Jesus' Command: Wait, Then Go! (4-8)
    3. The Ascension (9-11)

II. *Praying for the Spirit* (1:12-26)

    1. United in Prayer (12-14)
    2. The First Church Business Meeting (15-22)
    3. Matthias Succeeds Judas (23-26)

III. *The Coming of the Spirit* (2:1-41)

    1. The Promise Fulfilled (1-4)
    2. Each in His Own Language (5-13)
    3. A Tongue Touched by the Spirit (14-36)
    4. Three Thousand Converts! (37-41)

CHAPTER I

EMPOWERED BY THE SPIRIT

Acts 1:1 to 2:41

A modern New Testament church must be made up of baptized believers. Then the basic condition for its effective ministry is that it be empowered by the Spirit. Nothing can take the place of that endowment. Without it, the finest church building is only a monument to a contractor's skill; the most comprehensive organization of educational and missionary efforts will be but a futile scheme; and no leadership, however brilliant or winsome, can guide that church in accomplishing God's will. On the other hand, when empowered by the Spirit, a church of any size can use even an inadequate building to the glory of God, can win the lost and train the saved for effective witnessing through the church, and will discover a leadership whose vision and wisdom are works of the Spirit. Twentieth-century Baptist churches must be empowered by the Spirit if they would follow the New Testament pattern.

I. THE PROMISE OF THE SPIRIT (1:1-11)

During the precious hours on the eve of his crucifixion Jesus told his disciples several times of the Spirit whom the Father would send to strengthen and instruct them and to convict the world. Because the disciples did not realize what would happen to the Master so soon, they probably did not at that time understand the significance of his promise of the Spirit. Even though on the day after the crucifixion they may have recalled Jesus' reference to the Comforter, their joy in his resurrection probably veiled again their memory of that promised Spirit. Here in the opening verses of Acts we find a reiteration of that promise. But this time it is in a new context: the Saviour of men had been crucified, but he had conquered death; he faced a final earthly separation in the ascension. Again he promised the Spirit—this time to empower his followers for witnessing to the uttermost part of the earth.

1. From the Gospel to Acts (1-3)

Luke addressed his Gospel to "most excellent Theophilus." Since the word in Greek means God-lover, it is possible that he used the word as a general address to any lover of God. But the more probably explanation is that Theophilus was a real person, perhaps a friend and sponsor of the author. The words "most excellent" suggest that Theophilus may have been either noble or rich.

Luke at once reminded Theophilus of the Gospel he had previously written. He wanted him to understand that even with its glorious climax in Luke 24:50-53, the Gospel had a sequel. It was only the story of what "Jesus *began* both to do and to teach." When he wrote Acts, Luke knew that what Jesus had begun to do and to teach up to the time of his ascension he had continued to accomplish through Spirit-filled followers in the second half of that first century.

To make clear the continuity between his Gospel and Acts, Luke summarized in these opening verses the trend of events after the resurrection. He had closed his Gospel with references to five post-resurrection appearances of Jesus. In Acts he testified again to the reality of Jesus' resurrection. Furthermore, Luke pointed out that before the ascension Jesus had, through the power of the Holy Spirit, given commandments—probably the several commissions—to his chosen apostles and had continued to teach them about the kingdom of God.

Thus, Luke made his transition from the Gospel to Acts.

2. Jesus' Command: Wait, Then Go! (4-8)

The last time Jesus met with his disciples, perhaps in the upper room, he commanded them not to leave Jerusalem but to "wait for the promise of the Father." We are reminded in verse 5 of the statement made by John the Baptist in Matthew 3:11. John had used baptism with water as a symbol of revolutionary repentance, and Jesus had commanded baptism with water to symbolize the whole conversion experience of the individual. But here Jesus seems to have been saying that to perform the work for which he had called them his apostles must be saturated with the Spirit. (Of course in both instances "baptize" means immerse.) This baptism in the Spirit was not pictured as something that they could earn or merit; rather was it to be the gift of God "not many days hence."

With the promise of great spiritual power soon to be fulfilled and a commission weighing upon them to preach Christ to every creature, the apostles appear limited in their vision when at the last earthly meeting with their Lord they asked him frankly about the re-establishment of the kingdom of Israel. It is easy to be critical at this distance in time; but had we been in their places, few of us would have done differently. After all, the Jews had been subjects of Rome for nearly a century. They chafed at the continued domination an immorality of the conqueror. Jesus put an end to their questioning—and some modern questioning, too—in a firm statement that the times and the seasons which are under the authority of God are not the concern of his sons.

Much more important than trying to determine the dates in God's great plan are the power that Jesus promised and the program he projected in verse 8. Here is enough to keep the apostles busy for the rest of their lives, and here's the power to see it through! Indeed, this comes nearer than any other to being the key verse of the whole book of Acts. In a very real way it furnishes an outline for the whole book and for all Christian missions in succeeding centuries. Chosen witnesses are still going in Christ's name "unto the uttermost part of the earth." This ascension commission furnished a formula for missionary and evangelistic work; it has been the rallying cry for the whole missionary program—local, home, and foreign.

These are the words of One who in his earthly ministry was never more than forty miles outside his native land. This was a great vision of world conquest. But, of course, he wasn't just a man; as the Son of God he understood the purposes of God and he knew God's power. Some still might object that he was expecting too much of his mere human followers. The scope of Jesus' ministry was probably the measure of their own contact with the world; and since they were only human, they did not have Jesus' insight into the depth and breadth of the purposes of God. That objection, however, is stilled almost before it is raised; for implicit in Jesus' promise of the Spirit is all the vision, wisdom, and power that devoted followers would need to declare the message of salvation from Jerusalem to the world's last frontier.

Therefore, we see the necessity of Jesus' command: Wait, then go! For unless his apostles waited for the enduement of the Spirit, they would not be able to go in the power of the Spirit. The modern Christian is restrained by exactly the same command—restrained only that his going might be more effective.

3. *The Ascension (9-11)*

With these three verses we come to the close of the parallel material of the Gospel and Acts. The Gospel account pictures Jesus as leading his apostles from the upper room in Jerusalem out of the city toward Bethany. (The actual translation is "over against" Bethany.) But here in verse 12 we read that the apostles after the ascension "returned . . . from the mount called Olivet," which must have been the scene of the ascension. Luke pictures the ascension in Acts as if it occurred just as soon as Jesus gave his command about waiting for the Spirit and going into the world as his witnesses. Even while the apostles may have been framing some question or comment on that commission, Jesus "was taken up; and a cloud received him out of their sight."

Of course the ascension was a miracle and beyond our comprehension. The first-century Christians did not quibble about it. Many of them had seen Jesus alive before the crucifixion, and at least 500 of them had seen him after the resurrection; but we have no record of anyone who claimed to have seen Jesus except in some glorified state (experiences of Stephen and Paul) after the ascension. The ascension was the climax of the sublime facts of the incarnation.

Even in this experience the apostles were not left comfortless. For while they stood staring into the heavens where their Lord had disappeared, two men in white apparel stood by them and more or less recalled them from their preoccupation. These angelic messengers gave that bewildered disciple band some news that turned their sorrow into hope, that exchanged blessed memories for joyful anticipation. Their Lord and Master had left them but had promised his Spirit as their constant companion. Their Lord and Master had left them, but he would come again even as they had seen him go.

II. Praying for the Spirit (1:12-26)

Jesus had promised the Spirit to the waiting disciples. As they waited on the Lord, they waited in his courts: "continually in the temple, praising and blessing God" (Luke 24:53) and praying with one mind for the Spirit in their own meeting place. Modern Christians are still subject to the ascension commission. But before they rush off to win a lost neighbor or to dedicate themselves or substance for full-time mission service, they also must wait on the Lord and pray for his Spirit.

1. United in Prayer (12-14)

Really, "the acts of the apostles" began when those eleven men turned away from Mount Olivet and walked slowly toward Jerusalem. Luke described them in his Gospel as returning "to Jerusalem with great joy" (24: 52), and certainly they must have talked along the way, marveling at the things they had just seen and probably questioning one another as to the meaning of Jesus' final command.

When they re-entered the city, they went to the place where they had been accustomed to gather, "an upper room." It may have been the same upper room in which Jesus had led his disciples in celebrating the Passover and in which they had first partaken of the Lord's Supper. If it was in the home of a friend, as we suppose, it would have been quite natural for the apostles to return to it, not only in the blackness of their sorrow after the crucifixion, but also in the unexpected joys of sublime fellowship with the risen Christ. Verse 13 could mean that the room was the residence of the eleven apostles, but it probably means that the room had become during the forty days after the resurrection a sort of retreat for the apostles, a focus of prayer and fellowship.

Others than the apostles gathered in that upper room for prayer. Devoted women who had proved their love and loyalty for Jesus, Mary the mother of Jesus, and "his brethren" were there. Mary was probably still pondering many things in her heart, but she had seen and felt enough to know that her first-born was the Messiah and the Son of God. "His brethren" has been interpreted by some as his kinsmen or followers. But there is no reason for trying to ignore the fact that Jesus had some half brothers. True, they did not believe in him even as late as six months before the crucifixion (John 7:5); but they were changed, like many another, by the unanswerable testimony of the cross and the empty tomb. One, James, would later become leader of the Jerusalem church; another, Jude, would write a letter of encouragement to Christians under fire.

But the most significant thing about this brief passage is found in verse 14: "These all continued with one accord in prayer and supplication." Jesus had assigned them a gigantic task, but neither their enthusiasm for the gospel nor devotion to the Master led them to set to work before they were empowered from above. They did not know when that power would come. That was not their concern, for Jesus had set them straight on the times and seasons of the Father. They were willing to wait, and their waiting was not wasted. For them, waiting on the Lord meant communing with him in prayer. Theirs was a prayer meeting that lasted ten days.

It was not just the work of some leader, for Luke tells us that they prayed "with one accord"; however large the company, they had the same mind or spirit in prayer. Furthermore, their praying was much more than a form or a mouthing of words. To give the full force of the original word we ought to add "steadfastly" after "continued" in verse 14. But better still is the word picture suggested by Dr. Carver with the literal meaning of the original word: "apply their strength to prayer."

2. The First Church Business Meeting (15-22)

In the midst of their praying the disciples became aware of a practical problem for strengthening their ministry. Peter called it to their attention one day before Pentecost when all the Jerusalem believers, approximately 120, were gathered for fellowship and prayer. These evidently were the fruits of Jesus' ministry in Jerusalem. Their loyalty and devotion were recognized, and they were willing to be known as followers of the Nazarene. In those days following the ascension they probably grew more aware of themselves as the recipients and bearers of a great message. They doubtless felt their responsibility for unity and continuity within the group. Theirs was a fellowship that depended more upon a common loyalty than upon organization. They were the first church in Jerusalem.

To the Jerusalem church, then, in its first business meeting, Peter presented the problem of selecting a successor for Judas Iscariot in the circle of the apostles. Since the Old Testament was the Bible of the early Christians, it was natural for Peter to quote it in relation to Judas. His disloyalty and fatal betrayal had probably stunned the eleven. News of his suicide accentuated their horror and revulsion. They recalled Jesus' own use of a passage in Psalms to describe his betrayer (John 13:18).

Inspired writers pictured his deed and doom, but Judas made his own choice. His opportunities for fellowship with Christ had been no less than most of the disciple band. "He was numbered among us," Peter said, "and received his portion in this ministry" (ASV). Surely, until the very last, Jesus must have yearned to turn him from his desperate plan. After all, he *was* one of the twelve and had been chosen to declare the gospel. But the tense itself of Peter's sentence is the saddest comment on the career of Judas Iscariot: "He *was* numbered with us."

Since Jesus had chosen twelve as his disciples, Peter felt that the number should be kept intact. Thus he proposed that another apostle be selected. The candidates should be men who had been with the Master and the twelve throughout Jesus' earthly ministry up to the day of his ascension. Notice the event in Jesus' life which Peter thought should be the key to the gospel witness: "to be a witness with us of his resurrection."

3. Matthias Succeeds Judas (23-26)

When Peter had presented the problem and the way he thought it might be solved, the church began to review its membership to discover those who could qualify for the office. Two men were nominated. Then the church prayed for the guidance of the Lord in selecting one of these to be counted as one of the apostles. The first church in Jerusalem really believed in prayer. The Spirit had not come upon them, but they had a sense of vital fellowship with God. They knew that he was concerned with the progress of the work which they had been commissioned to do. But they did not take that concern for granted. As they prayed, they revealed their confidence that the Lord had already chosen the right man; they prayed that he might reveal his choice to them.

"Casting lots" was an accepted custom among the Jews for determining the will of Jehovah. It was natural that these Jewish Christians should use that device for determining the name of the new apostle. According to our records, however, the practice of casting lots in church action was never used after the coming of the Spirit at Pentecost. Some scholars suggest that the meaning of the

Greek word for "was numbered with" suggests an election, that Matthias was *voted* into the apostles' circle. However he was chosen, he was the Lord's choice for the place which Judas had renounced in order "to proceed into the place that was his very own" (Carver, 21).

III. THE COMING OF THE SPIRIT (2:1-41)

Without the Spirit's coming, there would have been no book of Acts. Not even the apostles would have had the power and wisdom to give a telling witness. They could recall many things from the deeds and teachings of Jesus. With the conviction and enthusiasm of eyewitnesses they could paint word pictures of his tragic crucifixion, his triumphant resurrection, his wondrous ascension. They were bound to one another in one fellowship through their love for Christ and his love for them. But Jesus knew that even these great lessons would not be sufficient for the task to which he had called them. Therefore, he promised them power from on high, an infilling of God's wisdom, strength, courage, and vision. The Holy Spirit would be their Comforter, Teacher, Advocate, Guide, and Challenger.

In the echo of that promise the apostles left the scene of ascension with great joy. United in mind and heart, they prayed for God's strength and guidance, for his courage and understanding. They prayed for the Spirit.

1. The Promise Fulfilled (1-4)

Both promise and prayer were filled full on Pentecost. That was the day, the fiftieth after the Passover, when the loyal Jews celebrated the completion of the grain harvest. Thus it was a time of thanksgiving and joy, and Jews from all around the Mediterranean came to Jerusalem to observe it. That is all that the day meant to the believers in Jerusalem as they gathered in the upper room on the sabbath (our Saturday). We have no reason to believe that they expected the coming of the Spirit on Pentecost. It was just another day of prayer and fellowship for them.

While they were gathered in that room before nine o'clock in the morning, a great thing happened to them. Suddenly the Spirit came upon them. His coming was demonstrated in two physical tokens: first, there was a sound "like the rush of a mighty wind, and it filled all the house where they were sitting" (RSV); second, there came a visible visitation to the head of each disciple of tongues that looked like fire. The original Greek gives the picture, not of a cloven tongue on each, but "the fire-like appearance presented itself at first, as it were, in a single body, and then suddenly parted in this direction and that; so that a portion of it rested on each of those present" (Hackett, 42).

Just as the Lord was not in the wind, the earthquake, or the fire at the mouth of Elijah's cave, neither was the Spirit in the sound of wind or the firelike tongues. To Elijah he spoke in a still, small voice after the manifestation of his power; for the disciples the marvelous sound and sight were but signs and symbols of the Spirit's coming. No naturalistic explanation is adequate for this great event. A third sign of the Spirit's coming was given in the disciples' ability to speak in other tongues. These three evidences of the Spirit's coming are just more than we can explain outside the realm of the miraculous.

Even more difficult to explain is the coming itself, attested by many lifetimes of Spirit-empowered witnessing. To argue that such an event was impossible because it has no equal in previous or subsequent history is no argument at all. If Luke is accepted as a trustworthy historian and interpreter of the early years of Christianity, then he must be accepted in this instance also. Those early disciples were impressed by the signs they saw and heard, but what impressed them more was the gift they had received. The visible signs seem almost to have been forgotten, but the Spirit's presence continued warm, vital, and invigorating.

2. Each in His Own Language (5-13)

Of course it may have been the sound "as of a rushing mighty wind" that attracted the attention of men outside the upper room; or it may have been the excitement and exultation of the disciples as they tested their gift of tongues. The latter seems more likely; for certainly those Spirit-empowered men and women could have taken calmly the gift which they had received. Theirs had been no ordinary experience; they were gripped by a power which had possessed their personalities. They recognized the sublime fulfilment of Jesus' promise and the answer to their own prayers. They may have shouted their joy, sung loudly their praise, and offered exuberant thanksgiving and fervent petition in prayer to the Lord.

Whatever it was that attracted their attention, "the multitude came together, and they were bewildered, because each one heard them speaking in his own language" (RSV). Now this was no ordinary crowd in a cosmopolitan center on a holiday. Devout Jews "out of every nation under heaven" made up this crowd. Some had come to celebrate Pentecost, some for pilgrimages, some to spend their last days in the holy city. From the lands beyond the Jordan, from Asia, from Egypt, from Italy— whether Jews or proselytes—all heard "the wonderful works of God" in their own tongue.

Of course it was a human thing to do, but notice that these men marveled first not at the message but at the way it was delivered. That they understood the basic Jewish traditions and were acquainted somewhat with the Old Testament is obvious from the way Peter preached. Hearing the message in their native tongue may have reminded them of the powers of ancient prophets, but they were not used to seeing and hearing 120 people speak like prophets. No wonder "all were amazed and perplexed, saying to one another, 'What does this mean?'" (RSV).

But some people always have an answer. If they can't explain an event, they attempt to explain it away. Most of the crowd seems to have realized that a miracle had taken place, but "others mocking said, These men are full of new wine."

3. A Tongue Touched by the Spirit (14-36)

Because of the reference to the "multitude" and to the large number of converts, as well as the reference to the apostles' worshiping in the Temple (Luke 24:53), some have thought that the Spirit must have come during a prayer service in the Temple area and that Peter preached to the hosts there. But Luke did not say that this great host of converts was the harvest of one sermon or of even a two-hour service. Evangelism on the first Pentecost must have continued throughout the day. For men and women possessed by the Holy Spirit as that group was would not rest with one evangelistic service. It would have been only a springboard for scores of personal soul-winning interviews and street corner services.

In the face of the bewilderment and mockery of Jews from the whole Empire, a fisherman stood up to claim the promise of Jesus that "the Holy Spirit shall teach you in that very hour what ye ought to say" (Luke 12:12 ASV). It was not unusual for him to be the spokesman for the apostles. His impulsiveness had often led him into trouble, but his sermon at Pentecost revealed a more mature apostle. His vigor and courage were unabated, but his tact and judgment and logic were like shining new facets of a gem in the polishing.

After courteously and earnestly addressing his congregation, Peter refuted the mockers easily. Since it was nine o'clock in the morning, these men would not be drunk. Moreover, devout Jews "were in the habit of fasting until after that hour on a feast day, nine being an 'hour of prayer' " (Carver, 28). Peter quickly gave the real explanation of the disciples' speaking in tongues. He called it a fulfilment of Joel's prophecy. That prophet of the ninth century before Christ had declared that in the last days ("the day of the Lord") God would pour out his Spirit upon both young and old, both men and women. No longer would the prophet, the king, the judge be the only ones peculiarly endowed. Others would be empowered to prophesy for God.

Certainly part of the prophecy had not been fulfilled (vv. 19-20), but Peter drove home his point that a new day had dawned in God's relationship to his people. A new invitation was being issued to all flesh: "Whosoever shall call on the name of the Lord shall be saved."

This was only the first step in Peter's explanation. Even though his hearers might accept the gift of tongues as a fulfilment of the passage from Joel, they would then ask: But what is the occasion or who is the agent of the Spirit's coming? The answer to this question is, of course, the heart of Peter's sermon. First, he reminded them of the wonderful works and signs that God accomplished through Jesus of Nazareth, which things showed God's approval of him. Then he made an awful accusation: Within the plan and foreknowledge of God those "men of Israel" had by the hands of lawless men crucified Jesus. But even so terrible an accusation was made more damning by Peter's next statement: "God raised him up" (RSV). It was bad enough to kill an innocent man, a man who had accomplished many wonderful things by God's help. But when God raised that man up, he brought an awful judgment against those who had killed him.

To underscore his testimony to the resurrection, Peter appealed to the authority of David (Psalm 16:8-11). David could not have been speaking of himself; for David died, "and his tomb is with us unto this day" (ASV)— evidence enough that he had never been raised to life. Empowered as a prophet, David was not speaking of himself but of his descendant who would succeed to his throne —the Messiah, or Christ. And Jesus of Nazareth was that one whose soul could not remain in the place of disembodied spirits and whose flesh did not decay. Then perhaps with a gesture to include the eleven disciples standing with him, Peter declared boldly, "This Jesus that hath God raised up, whereof we all are witnesses."

In the next verse Peter returned to his explanation of the disciples' gifts of tongues; it was poured forth by the exalted Christ through his Spirit. With one further reference to David (Psalm 110:1), Peter came to the climax of his sermon. This Jesus of Nazareth whom the men of Israel had crucified was by all these evidences the Christ of God—a solemn declaration for every Jewish ear!

4. Three Thousand Converts! (37-41)

Through the words and presence of Peter, the Spirit had been accomplishing his convicting work in the hearts of that crowd on the first Christian Pentecost. The Greek word is stronger than the connotation of our word "pricked"; it could mean pierced, cut, or stunned. Peter's accusation was so convincing that some of the very people who had cried out for Jesus' crucifixion were now imploring the apostles: "What shall we do?"

Peter knew that his words had struck home, that the time had come for a ringing invitation to acknowledge Jesus as Saviour and Lord. But he did not make it easy; he declared requirements consistent with Jesus' own message and commission. First, he called for repentance. That was basic in the preaching of Jesus as he called for a complete change in mind and in life. No matter how beautiful or logical one's ideas may be about God, one cannot find peace and fellowship with him without changing one's mind and behavior with reference to sin and to God. To repent, man must go beyond sorrow or regret; and repent he *must* if he is to begin to find the answer to the dilemma of conviction.

Second, this change of attitude must be followed by the acceptance of Jesus Christ as Saviour and Lord, symbolized by baptism in his name. Thus they would not only memorialize publicly an inner experience, but they would through baptism be declaring their allegiance to his cause as represented in the church. Then they, too, would receive the gift of the Holy Spirit. For the promise of Joel included Peter's congregation, their children, and "all that are afar off"—even the Gentiles.

That wasn't all of Peter's challenging invitation; for "with many other words he testified and exhorted them, saying, Save yourselves from this crooked generation" (ASV). We don't know how long the service lasted or what part the other apostles played in it. We don't know how the multitude made known their individual decisions to accept Christ. Undoubtedly the majority of the 120 persons in the disciple band must have given themselves to personal testimony throughout that day. Of course many claimed Christ as Saviour at the invitation of Peter, and they were baptized. Verse 41 may mean that "about three thousand souls" responded to that one invitation. "Whether they were all baptized that very day we are not told, nor does it seem important that we shall know. Nothing appears to the contrary. The time has passed when there is any need among informed men to show the possibility of baptizing so great a number" (Carver, 34).

The remarkable fact was, not that three thousand could be won and baptized, but that God's Spirit had indeed empowered about one hundred and twenty followers of Jesus so that with the Spirit's help they could win three thousand others to faith in Christ. This was no ordinary occurrence arising out of man's ingenuity; this was a miracle wrought in and through human personality by a divine entrance for the eternal purpose of God.

For Review and Further Study

1. What were the signs of the Spirit's coming at Pentecost? What is the basic evidence of the Spirit's coming in any Christian's life?

2. Who made up the company of believers between the ascension and Pentecost? How many were there?

3. In selecting a successor to Judas, what did Peter urge as the key to the gospel witness?

4. Confident of the resurrection of Christ, the disciples had great and good news to tell the world. Why did they need a visitation of the Spirit?

5. Who heard Peter's sermon at Pentecost? How did they respond to it?

6. Outline briefly Peter's sermon. Find his explanation, accusation, and invitation.

7. What did the disciples probably do after Peter's sermon?

II

TESTED IN FELLOWSHIP

Acts 2:42 to 5:42

I. *Discovering a New Community* (2:42-47)

II. *Declaring the Gospel in Service and Sermon* (3:1-26)

    1. A Miracle at the Gate (1-10)
    2. Peter Preaches in the Temple (11-26)

III. *Standing Firm Before Opposition* (4:1-31)

    1. The Arrest and Defense of the Apostles (1-12)
    2. The Verdict of the Court (13-22)
    3. The Prayer of the Church (23-31)

IV. *Exploring a New Stewardship* (4:32 to 5:11)

    1. Barnabas Sets an Example (4:32-37)
    2. Two Gave for Self-glory (5:1-11)

V. *Giving First Obedience to God* (5:12-42)

    1. Jealous Sadducees Arrest the Apostles (12-28)
    2. Peter's Defense and Gamaliel's Advice (29-39)
    3. The Apostles Continue Their Preaching (40-42)

TESTED IN FELLOWSHIP

Acts 2:42 to 5:42

"Money is not important," a deacon said to his pastor. "If the people are committed to Christ and to one another, they can do anything they are supposed to do as a church."

Church members who really love the Lord and one another won't let anything—money, building, or community customs—prevent them from achieving the ultimate purposes of their church. Once empowered by the Spirit, they will prove their salvation and enduement through active participation in the life and work of the church which Jesus founded.

In this fellowship of Christians they will test their knowledge of Christian principles for right living and share their joy in Christ and their enthusiasm for the kingdom. Thus, in Christian experience fellow church members become one body—"one in hope and doctrine, one in charity." In that fellowship they share one another's joys and sorrows; they work together, each in his own way, in declaring the gospel and building up the church; they resist as one man the inroads of evil and the invitation to compromise their loyalty. Our twentieth-century world still needs Christians and churches empowered by the Spirit and tested in fellowship.

I. Discovering a New Community (2:42-47)

Settling on a date for the origin of the first church of Jesus Christ is even more difficult than trying to determine when a man begins to build a house. Does he begin to build only when the rock foundation is laid? Was not the excavation the beginning? Or did he begin when he first selected his materials? What about the rough sketches and the finished blueprints? Or can we ignore the house he saw with his mind's eye when he first bought the lot on the knoll? When does a man begin to build a house?

God had a plan for his people, a plan of reconciliation and fellowship. Jesus called a few men out from the crowds and gave them special training. On the basis of their bold declaration of faith in him as the Son of God, he promised to build his church. That first church was but the thought of God. No group of men and women set themselves to organize it; it emerged—a divine-human fellowship—out of the walks and talks of a few men and women with Jesus Christ, their Saviour.

Of course Acts tells the story of that first church and of others in Asia and Europe. In 1:8 we heard the church commissioned; in 1:14 we found the church at prayer; in 2:4 we felt the church empowered for its work; and in 2:41 we saw the church grow by "about three thousand souls." The church lost none of its evangelistic fervor in adding so many to its fellowship. One or two other changes did take place.

Most of these new converts knew very little about the teachings of Jesus; therefore, they had to be instructed that they might bear an effective witness. As they began to understand the meaning of Jesus' words, they also needed some help in entering upon the Way which he had pioneered. They would have to discover the Christian community. In all these things verse 42 tells us that the apostles led the new converts. Certainly "the apostles' doctrine" does not suggest that the new converts had memorized any formal statement of theological dogma.

"Doctrine" here just means teaching or instruction. No real Christian community or church can be built without that kind of teaching.

Foolish men used to think that it didn't make any difference what you believed so long as you believed something. But the world's most disastrous war was fought, not because some vicious people believed nothing, but because they believed something so hideous that the rest of the world risked life and wealth to prevent its spread.

The church was not first a school, however; it was and is basically a fellowship, a community of baptized believers. Thus each new convert had to be led to find his own place in the church as a fellow believer and a child of God. That is probably the significance of their continuing steadfastly in "fellowship." Verse 42 suggests two ways by which that might have been achieved: "in breaking of bread, and in prayers." We cannot be absolutely certain what is meant by "in breaking of bread." It can mean the Lord's Supper, meals which the disciples ate together, or the Lord's Supper following such a common meal. In the light of verse 46, the last explanation seems more probable.

Fellowship was enhanced also by their prayer life. Devout Jews knew something about prayer; they said their prayers at home and went frequently to the Temple for prayer periods. But those devout Jews who on Pentecost acknowledged Jesus as their Saviour and Lord discovered in the Christian community a new enthusiasm for, and facility in, praying. They went to the Temple daily; they held their own services in first one home and then another; in the gift of the Spirit they discovered new power through personal prayer.

Doubtless because there were many poor people in that first church, a generous but short-lived practice of sharing the wealth of the community was begun. In verse

44 we are reminded that all believers "were together" which may mean that they were united in spirit or that they had appointed a central meeting place, a sort of general headquarters. At least, some arrangement was made for receiving and distributing funds and goods to the needy. From the tenses of verbs in verses 44-45 we understand that "the sales of real estate and of personal property were made by the owners from time to time and the distribution was made on the basis of need as the need developed" (Carver, 35). This distribution, then, was not communism, nor was it just the desperate action of believers who expected the immediate end of the age.

All that was done appealed favorably to all the people; they discovered a new community in their midst. By the power of the Spirit, that community gave its testimony, "and the Lord added to their number day by day those who were being saved" (RSV).

II. DECLARING THE GOSPEL IN SERVICE AND SERMON (3:1-26)

No date can be set positively for any of the events, except for Pentecost, in the first eight chapters of Acts. Included with certain summaries like 2:42-47 are a number of incidents which dramatize the spread of Christianity from A.D. 29 to 33 (or 35), the generally accepted date for Paul's conversion. The healing of the lame man at the gate Beautiful may have been recounted to illustrate the "many wonders and signs . . . done by the apostles" (2:43). It was a most significant incident because it led to the first clash of the Christians with Jewish authorities.

1. A Miracle at the Gate (1-10)

Peter and John were evidently the leaders of the Jerusalem church during its first few years. Yet when the two went up to the Temple for the three o'clock prayer service, they still showed themselves loyal Jews.

Since the gate Beautiful is not so called again in the Testament or in contemporary literature, we cannot be sure just where it was located. But it was probably the eastern (and main) entrance to the Temple proper, entering the court of the women from the court of the Gentiles. That would be a suitable place for a crippled beggar. From the tense of the verb we get the idea that he was just being placed at his regular stand when the two apostles arrived at the gate. He asked of them what he asked of all who passed by.

How disappointing must have been Peter's first words to him! What did they think he was sitting there for if not to receive a piece of silver or gold? With what else could one buy bread? Fine speeches could not satisfy a gnawing appetite or clothe a man against the evening chill. And what could these men give that would be better than silver or gold? Then suddenly he heard a strange invocation and command: "In the name of Jesus Christ of Nazareth, walk" (RSV). That name was familiar. Perhaps he had seen Jesus in the Temple once; he may have heard stories of his mighty works and wished that the Healer might come his way. Then without warning, Peter grasped the beggar by his hand and pulled him to his feet, "and immediately his feet and ankles were made strong" (RSV).

The time for questions and complaints had passed. Hilariously testing his God-given strength, the man walked with the apostles into the Temple. Since it was the hour of prayer, it had always been a profitable time for him. But on that day he turned it into the hour of praise. Asking for some money for the day, he had received his limbs for life. Begging a boon in the name of charity, he had received in the name of Jesus Christ something which money could not buy. That name stood for all Jesus Christ had been and was continuing to be through the ministry of his followers empowered by his Spirit. In his name—by his power—the lame are still made to walk, the blind receive their sight, the selfish turn their wealth to world need, the immoral find purity, the lost are saved!

2. Peter Preaches in the Temple (11-26)

What a joyous time it was for the healed beggar! Whatever decorum he knew, he forgot it as he walked and leaped and shouted his praises to God; and between bounds he grabbed the clothing and arms of the apostles to express his gratitude. Of course, such a commotion aroused the wonder and curiosity of other worshipers, and they thronged around the three men in Solomon's Porch. This was a colonnade built along the inside of the eastern wall of the Temple area.

Doubtless the crowd was raising questions; they could hardly have been still after seeing such a miracle. Whether they were just generally clamorous or directed their questions specifically at Peter, the apostle attempted to answer them. First of all, he emphasized their wonderment by asking why they should marvel. Then he attempted to erase from their minds any thought that the apostles themselves by their own "power or piety" (Carver) had accomplished the feat. Perhaps pausing momentarily to let his question sink in, Peter then launched into the real explanation of the miracle.

As on Pentecost, Peter had again to introduce Jesus, but this time he did it more directly and boldly. He identified himself with his hearers by the way he referred to Jehovah: "The God of our fathers." Then he brought his same terrible accusation against his hearers. They had delivered Jehovah's servant Jesus unto Pilate. ("Son" is not the best translation here.) Then when Pilate had made up his mind to release Jesus, they denied him before Pilate and asked that a murderer be released instead. Thus, they killed the "Prince of Life." (The word for "Prince" is translated as guide, author, and pioneer in several modern versions of the New Testament.)

But the Prince of life could not be held by death; Peter and John were witnesses of his resurrection. And it was because of faith in the risen Christ—the faith of the cripple and the faith of the apostles—that the lame man had been made strong.

While the terrible accusation was still ringing in their ears, the people heard Peter begin a sympathetic appeal. The prophets foretold what the Christ should suffer, and these things had been fulfilled. Through suffering God "glorified his servant Jesus" (v. 13 RSV). Recalling what he had suffered and recognizing him as the promised Messiah, the Jews were called upon to repent that their sins might be erased and that new blessings might come from Jehovah. The greatest of these would be sending "the Christ who hath been appointed for you, even Jesus" (ASV).

To illustrate his argument, Peter quoted from Moses (Deut. 18:15-16, 19) and from the covenant of God with Abraham (Gen. 22:18), perhaps two of the many passages which Jesus made clear to his disciples after his resurrection. (See Luke 24:27, 44-45.)

In the last verse Peter seems to have been drawing close to an "invitation." The Suffering Servant of God had been killed, but God had raised him up again. He had been sent to the Jews first; indeed, he himself was a Jew. He had come with a blessing for them "in turning every one of you from your wickedness" (RSV). This was a powerful appeal. Perhaps it wasn't a sermon according to our modern standards, but it was a well-informed and passionate witness for Christ to "men of Israel."

III. STANDING FIRM BEFORE OPPOSITION (4:1-31)

We are not left in doubt as to the results of that afternoon sermon. In 4:4 we read that "many of those who heard the word believed; and the number of the men came to about five thousand" (RSV). On Pentecost the church grew from about 120 to about 3,000 members. We cannot say positively that the sermon in Solomon's Porch won another 2,000 converts; we do not know anything about the evangelistic efforts since Pentecost. Doubtless the church had been growing gradually in the intervening days or weeks. But the very fact that no other great harvest of souls between Pentecost and this occasion was recounted by Luke seems to indicate that all or most of the 2,000 increase came as a result of Peter's Sermon in the Temple.

1. The Arrest and Defense of the Apostles (1-12)

Healing a man lame from birth and crediting the miracle to Jesus Christ of Nazareth brought many people to accept that Jesus as their Lord and Saviour. But it only annoyed "the priests, and the captain of the temple, and the Sadducees." The very people who should have been most interested in discovering the truth of God in prophecy and in Jesus were incensed because the apostles were "teaching the people and proclaiming in Jesus the resurrection from the dead" (RSV).

Really, the three groups mentioned were hardly more than one. There were the Sadducees—not all of them but enough to represent the party. There were the priests, most of whom were Sadducees; and there was the captain of the Temple guards, who probably found it convenient to side with his superiors. Thus, the Sadducees had their way. As the aristocratic rationalists among the Jewish leadership, they were opposed to allowing untrained men to teach people, especially when they declared the resurrection of the dead. Against that doctrine all Sadducees reacted violently.

When the disciples were arrested, they were probably locked in one of the rooms of the Temple because it was too late to have the trial that day. But next day there seems to have been a full meeting of the Sanhedrin, and Luke names a few of their leaders, two of whom we recall from the trials of Jesus. From verse 6 it is obvious that the Sanhedrin was quite a "family affair." Before this court of approximately seventy men the two apostles were called to answer the specific question: "By what power, or by what name, have ye done this?"

Empowered by the Spirit, Peter was ready with an answer. His accusers seem to have realized that something unusual had happened in the Temple, but they dared not name it. Calmly and respectfully Peter not only filled in the blanks of their question but gave it an answer as well. In the seats of honor he saw Annas and Caiaphas, and he remembered what they had done to Jesus, but unflinchingly he made the same declaration— terrible accusation and all—that he had made on other occasions. Then he remembered Jesus' own use of a passage from Psalms in dealing with some representatives of this very court. (See Matt. 21:42-45.) Instead of quoting Psalm 118:22, Peter made a direct application of it by changing "the builders" to "you builders."

Then Peter summed up his brief testimony in a sublime sentence. Here is the text for many a great sermon. Here's reason enough for staking one's life in a missionary venture across the sea or across the street. Even as the lame man had been made whole in the name of Jesus Christ of Nazareth, even so can all men find new life in Christ. He is not just *a* savior; he is the *only* Saviour of men. No matter who they are—crippled beggar or haughty Sadducee, untrained workman or brilliant scientist—if they are to be saved at all, it must be through Jesus Christ.

2. The Verdict of the Court (13-22)

The court was stunned by the apostle's testimony. "Actually Peter had turned the table on the Sanhedrin and had arraigned them before the bar of God" (Robertson, 51). Their vicious jealousy of Jesus of Nazareth, had come to haunt them, and they wondered how they might handle these new offenders. Who were they, anyway? Certainly they were bold in deed and in word. And they presented their case well even though obviously they had received no training in a rabbinical school. They were not professional teachers but laymen. (Instead of "ignorant" they were "common" men.) As the court made these observations and marveled, they began to realize that these two men had been with Jesus.

In the presence of the beggar healed in the name of Jesus "they had nothing to say in opposition" (RSV). Instead, they excused the apostles from the council chamber and conferred among themselves as to their verdict and sentence. What we have in verses 16-17 is perhaps only a summary of their discussion. Their only hope was to keep the news from spreading further among the people. But when they called the apostles in and "charged them not to speak or teach at all in the name of Jesus" (RSV), Peter and John had an answer for them. They sounded the note of the prophets' sense of urgency and divine guidance. Just as the Spirit had opened the eyes and touched the lips of those ancient

spokesmen for God, so had he empowered these new
heralds of the Christ: "We cannot but speak the things
which we have seen and heard." Before that affirmation
the Sanhedrin was impotent. The healing and teaching in
the Temple earned only threats now because "all men
praised God for what had happened" (RSV).

3. *The Prayer of the Church (23-31)*

What had the church been doing while two of their
leaders had been under arrest? Many of them were
probably gathered in their central meeting place and
were continuing in that activity which distinguished the
fellowship. Very likely some had prayed all night,
begging for the deliverance of Peter and John or entreat-
ing the Lord to teach them what to say before their accusers and strengthen them for any ordeal.

They knew their prayers were answered when the two
apostles reported all that had happened, especially the
demands and threats of the Sanhedrin. How easy it
would have been for the church to compromise, to agree
to be silent in the face of those threats. Perhaps some did
forsake the fellowship. But those gathered in the upper
room did not fear. Instead, they turned again to God in
prayer. And it is a wonderful prayer that Luke has saved
for us.

Addressing God as "Sovereign Lord" (RSV), they used
the language of Psalm 146:6 to ascribe their praise. Then
with the threatenings of the rulers still in their ears, they
recalled the inspired prediction of David concerning the
persecution of the Lord's Anointed *(Christos)*. And the
prophecy had been fulfilled in what men had done to
his "holy Servant Jesus" (ASV, instead of "holy child
Jesus"). In the light of these affirmations they made
their petition, not to save them from hurt, not to change
the mind of the Sanhedrin, not to give patience to wait

for a more expedient day, but: "Grant unto thy servants, that with all boldness they may speak thy word."

Their world was ruled by a whimsical emperor. Might measured right. Even the faith of their fathers was more interested in political advantage and religious technicalities than in finding and following the will of God. Yet these first-century Christians prayed only that they might be bold in their witness while God continued his work through them.

And God answered that prayer! An immediate sign was given when the place of prayer was shaken as if by an earthquake. Then came a fresh infilling by the Spirit of all those present, and they "spoke the word of God with boldness" (RSV). Thus when the Jerusalem church was tested in fellowship by persecution, it prayed only for strength to be better witnesses.

IV. EXPLORING A NEW STEWARDSHIP (4:32 to 5:11)

Contrary to the cynical judgment of the Preacher in the Old Testament (Eccl. 1:9c), the church of Jesus Christ *is* a new thing under the sun. Not even the congregation of Israel had brought the peace and joy to its members that Christians found in the fellowship of the Spirit. That fellowship has met many a test during these nineteen hundred years, but most of the tests were once met successfully by the first Jerusalem church. In prayer they really became a new kind of community. In the face of human need they brought healing to men's bodies and souls. Before opposition they stood firm. Next they must face a test within the fellowship—the test of a new stewardship.

1. Barnabas Sets an Example (4:32-37)

What a wonderful thing to say of any church: "The multitude of them that believed were of one heart and of one soul"! Together they prayed and praised God. But they did not stop with prayer and praise, for their fellowship with one another in Christ was so real that it affected both purse and property.

Already in 2:44 we have found the church making an adjustment to immediate needs as their fellowship grew rapidly. In this section, however, we have an enlarged account of this practice based on two Christian principles of stewardship and illustrated by two personal experiences. First, they seem to have realized that none of the things they possessed were really their own. All things came—and still come!—from the goodness of God. Thus they belong to him and to all his creatures. Second, whatever men possess, they are only its temporary users, tenants, or stewards. We come into this life with none of this world's goods; and when we leave, we can take nothing with us.

These first-century Christians took those principles so seriously that "they had everything in common" (RSV). Verses 32, 34-35 suggest a social ownership, but it was wholly different from the communism now in power in several countries. This Christian arrangement was wholly voluntary; it did not affect their democratic form of government; the tenses of the verbs indicate that it was an occasional practice rather than a rule of the community. As needs arose within the fellowship, the wealthier members would sell property and bring the money to the apostles for distribution to the poor according to their need. For various reasons we are confident that this practice did not continue long in first-century Christianity, but its basic principles continued to call forth sacrificial giving by the few and to challenge the many to explore a new stewardship.

One noble steward in that congregation is mentioned by name. He was Joseph, a native of Cyprus and a Levite who may have come rather early into Christian fellowship. At least the apostles knew him well enough to give him a very complimentary nickname. Since "Barnabas" was an Aramaic name, Theophilus would not understand its significance, and Luke gave its meaning in Greek: "son of exhortation (or consolation)."

Barnabas sold a field, whether in Cyprus or Palestine we do not know, and brought the money—the full sale price—"and laid it at the apostles' feet." As he set an example in his stewardship, this same Barnabas would set an example in evangelism and missions.

2. Two Gave for Self-glory (5:1-11)

Up to this point Luke has told nothing but good things about the Christian fellowship. We could wish that he never had anything else to tell, but even the first-century Christians were human. The inspired writers never ignored that human factor; they did not gloss over the sins and weaknesses of even the greatest Bible characters.

Luke does not tell us that Ananias and Sapphira explicitly stated that they were giving all the purchase price of their property to the needs of the church, but in Peter's accusation we understand that Ananias had tried to give that impression. Peter's questions revealed to both Ananias and the assembly the man's inescapable responsibility for his deed. He had not sinned in bringing only part of the sale price; he had sinned in pretending that his gift was more than it was. He and his wife wanted the praise of men for their generosity; but worse still, they misrepresented their gift to get that praise.

Peter's judgment, "Thou hast not lied unto men, but unto God," was more than Ananias could stand. Without word or warning he fell dead. Of course the church was horrified, but perhaps no more by Ananias' death than by the magnitude of his sin. Immediately some young men served as pallbearers for the body. "The time for burial was short in Jerusalem for sanitary reasons and to avoid ceremonial defilement" (Robertson, 60).

About three hours later Sapphira came to the meeting place of the church but did not know about the death of her husband. When Peter asked her whether they had sold the land for so much, she said yes. With his next question Peter let her know that he was aware of their conspiracy "to tempt the Spirit of the Lord." The judgment and punishment of God fell swiftly.

As that first church explored the practices and principles of a new stewardship, they were profoundly impressed by the judgment of God upon those who would make gifts for self-glory; at the same time they rejoiced in the generosity and thoughtfulness of other members. They were still being tested in fellowship, and only a few were found wanting.

V. GIVING FIRST OBEDIENCE TO GOD (5:12-42)

Testing days were not over; indeed, they had just begun. That praying church expected God to answer their petitions for boldness in witnessing. And he gave them boldness. In a world of sin, however, he could not guarantee physical protection from those who would come to hate both their boldness and their message.

1. Jealous Sadducees Arrest the Apostles (12-28)

Even though Luke did not give up any specific clues as to the time that was passing in his narrative, he did stop occasionally to summarize the general accomplishments and trends in that first-century church. Verses 12-16 offer one of these summaries. With about five thousand members in the fellowship, they could no longer use the upper room as their central meeting place, although it may have remained the prayer meeting room and the headquarters for the leaders. The followers of the Nazarene had become a significant force, and "the people held them in high honor" (RSV). While the idly curious and other unbelievers dared not join them, multitudes of true believers kept on being added to the Lord. In others words, the more Spirit-filled and pure the church, the more it will grow.

As the church grew, the apostles' ministry of healing also grew. People in Jerusalem even carried their sick into the streets, hoping that Peter's passing shadow might cure them. "There was, of course, no virtue or power in Peter's shadow. That was faith with superstition. . . . God honours even superstitious faith if it is real faith in him" (Robertson, 62). The fame of the apostles spread beyond Jerusalem, and the people of neighboring cities brought those sick in body and in mind, "and they were healed every one."

But it was in those very days of many triumphs over evil that official opposition took steps to silence the word and stay the work of the apostles. Filled with jealousy (preferable to "indignation"), the high priest and the Sadducees had the whole group of apostles arrested and put in jail. Evidently this arrest, too, occurred in the late afternoon and no trial was held immediately. The hesitation set the stage for a further delay in the trial.

For during the night an angel of the Lord delivered them from the prison and commanded them to go to the Temple and continue their teaching and preaching. Therefore, when the Sanhedrin (both "council" and "senate") called for their prisoners, the officers returned with an unbelievable story. While the court puzzled over their report and wondered how far the whole thing might go, someone rushed in with the news that the so-called prisoners were teaching in the Temple. When at last they stood before the Sanhedrin, the high priest reminded them in a question of the court's previous command. Then he revealed in a sort of accusation what the Sadducees must have felt to be the most dangerous theme in the apostles' preaching.

2. Peter's Defense and Gamaliel's Advice (29-39)

Against this serious charge Peter and the apostles defended themselves with an unanswerable utterance. It was much like the previous statement of Peter and John before the Sanhedrin in 4:19-20. These men were still living under the compulsion of the Spirit. With so keen a sense of the divine purpose being worked out through them, there was no real decision between obedience to God and obedience to mere men. "We ought to obey God rather than men."

That declaration has stiffened the courage of many a martyr; explained his endurance of the most terrible death; won to the cause of his Lord those who had found obedience to mere men a futile exercise. It has been the watchword of Baptists through many centuries.

Then to explain their conviction Peter gave practically the same testimony that he had given during the previous trial. He claimed that the accused apostles were through the powerful witness of the Spirit, witnesses themselves of these things. That's as far as Peter went. Suddenly the court exploded with rage. They "were cut to the heart," but not with pain or remorse. The Greek word here means to cut in two, and pictures a vicious rage. Some insisted on death for the apostles.

After the prisoners had been taken from the room, a Pharisee stood to defend them. Well, it seemed to be defense, for it did save the apostles from serious punishment. But really Gamaliel was demonstrating only a shrewd worldly wisdom and, at the same time, scoring a point against the Sadducees. Gamaliel was the grandson of the great Hillel, one of the leaders of the Pharisees. He was the teacher of Saul of Tarsus, who probably caught from Gamaliel some of the zeal he showed later in persecuting the Christians. Honored as a great rabbi, Gamaliel cannot be accounted in any way as sympathetic with the followers of Jesus. With the calmness of the scholar Gamaliel advised the court to consider carefully what they should do with the prisoners.

Then before announcing his principle of judgment, Gamaliel cited two proofs of its wisdom. Two different men had announced themselves as some kind of prophet, and each had drawn to himself a sizable group of followers. But in each case when the leader had been killed, the followers were scattered. Gamaliel hinted that these followers of Jesus were probably no different from these other bands who had lost their leaders. He counseled the Sanhedrin to let the apostles alone, "for if this plan or undertaking is of men, it will fail" (RSV). In that case the Sanhedrin would waste its concern over something that would fail anyway. On the other hand, if the apostles represented a movement blessed of God, they could not be stopped anyway. And if the Sanhedrin should oppose them, they "might even be found to be God-fighters" (Carver, 61).

3. The Apostles Continue Their Preaching (40-42)

The Sanhedrin accepted Gamaliel's advice, but the court did not feel that the apostles should be released without some punishment and another warning. After all, these men had flagrantly disobeyed an explicit command from the Sanhedrin.

The beating had a strange effect upon the apostles. Instead of bowing before the court and limping away dejectedly from their punishment, they were elated to be "counted worthy to suffer dishonor for the Name" (ASV). Doubtless they gave some evidence in conversation and conduct that the indignities they suffered at the hands of the Sanhedrin were really a fulfilment of their earnest desire to be true and happy witnesses to their Lord. They did not rejoice in the suffering, for that would have been a perversion of Jesus' standard for the kingdom man. (See Matt. 5:11-12.) They were not seeking martyrdom. They sought the privilege of loyalty to Christ at any cost.

Then instead of "enjoying" their satisfaction in suffering for Christ, they considered their conflict with the authorities as only an incident and continued with the work to which they had been called. Still believing that they should obey God rather than men, they returned to the Temple and went from house to house daily teaching and preaching "Jesus as the Christ" (Robertson). Their message was unchanged.

For Review and Further Study

1. In what ways are present-day churches tested in their fellowship?
2. List some practices of that first church in Jerusalem that made it different from every other organization.
3. How do we know that the early Christians' way of helping the poor was entirely different from modern communism?
4. Why is the teaching of beliefs so important in a church?
5. How was Peter's sermon on Solomon's Porch similar to his sermon at Pentecost?
6. What were the Sadducees' two reasons for having the apostles arrested after the lame man had been healed?
7. What was remarkable about the prayer of the church after Peter and John had been released by the Sanhedrin?
8. Suggest several great Christians who through the centuries tried to live by the apostles' principle in Acts 5:30.

III

ZEALOUS IN WITNESSING

Acts 6:1 to 8:40

I. *Chosen for Service* (6:1-7)

   1. Trouble in the Jerusalem Church **(1-4)**
   2. Seven Chosen to Serve (5-7)

II. *Serving as a Martyr* (6:8 to 8:1a)

   1. The Charges Against Stephen (6:8-15)
   2. Stephen's Defense (7:1-53)
      (1) Reviewing Hebrew History (1-50)
      (2) Condemning the Sanhedrin (51-53)
   3. The First Martyr (7:54 to 8:1a)

III. *Serving as a Missionary* (8:1b-40)

   1. The First Persecution (1b-4)
   2. Philip Preaches in Samaria (5-13)
   3. The Apostles Strengthen Philip's Work (14-25)
   4. Philip Wins the Ethiopian (26-40)

III

ZEALOUS IN WITNESSING

Acts 6:1 to 8:40

As the devoted followers of Christ prayed in the upper room, they were empowered by the Holy Spirit—empowered to obey the commission of their Lord. They had been called individually into his service, and each had personally committed himself in faith to the Christ. But in their devotion to him, they realized their relationship with one another, their unity in Christ.

In the days that followed their enduement they witnessed boldly to the risen Christ. Words alone would have accomplished very little. Unbelievers watched their lives. Once empowered by the Spirit, they began at once to witness by their words and their walk. They did not wait until they could call a new pastor, redecorate the church house, take a census, employ a visitation secretary, or complete the every-member canvass. Had they not received power for their world mission? Were they not of one mind toward Christ and toward one another? Even a twentieth-century church will be zealous in witnessing when it moves in the power of the Spirit and as one fellowship in Christ.

I. CHOSEN FOR SERVICE (6:1-7)

The titles for all nine chapters of this book characterize the entire story of Acts. Those early disciples were always zealous in witnessing. But in the first two chapters we have dealt with the witness of the apostles; in this chapter we become acquainted with a small and specially chosen group of workers who made a name for themselves in their devotion and diligence in declaring the gospel. Although they were not at this time called deacons (meaning servant or minister), they were chosen to serve and to minister. Their honesty, fairness, and concern for all helped maintain the fellowship of the Jerusalem Christians. That fellowship was a judgment against the exclusiveness of Judaism; it was a challenge to the cruel pagan world. Thus, those who helped maintain that fellowship were witnessing mightily to the Lord.

1. Trouble in the Jerusalem Church (1-4)

Church members are human beings. Even the members of that first Jerusalem church were still men and women. All who had acknowledged Christ as Saviour and Lord had become new creatures in him, but they were not wholly free from the littleness of the flesh. The gospel has never offered moral and spiritual perfection in this life. It is realistic in its attitude toward sin and its message of salvation. That's the reason Luke never hesitated to tell the full story of that first church; he knew that those early Christians were still in the process of becoming what God intended them to be.

Even while "the number of the disciples was multiplying" (ASV), a spirit of unrest arose in the church. Some of the members felt they weren't being treated fairly. Jewish Christians who were born outside of Palestine (usually called Grecians) complained that their widows were being neglected in the daily distribution of food and other necessities.

Instead of taking offense at this complaint, the apostles silently acknowledged its justice and proposed a plan to care for the situation. In good democratic fashion the whole church was called together and urged to select seven men to manage the fellowship affairs of the church. They were to be men of good reputation—an obvious and basic requirement for service in the church. But a good reputation is never enough; those seven were to be men who had given evidence of the indwelling Spirit and of the kind of wisdom necessary for their special task. What a wonderful set of qualifications for church service in any age!

In making this proposal the apostles were not trying to establish another order of Christian workers. They sought only to share their responsibility with some who would be officially selected by the church. They were wise in not trying to carry the whole load by themselves. Most modern churches need a greater division of labor. They were wise, too, in evaluating their own distinctive ministry. They had been the intimate followers of the Master; they had been specially trained by him for witnessing; they were recognized by the authorities as the leaders of the Christian group. Therefore they accepted their primary responsibility for preaching and teaching God's word in Christ.

2. Seven Chosen to Serve (5-7)

Undoubtedly the church was led of the Spirit to see the wisdom in the apostles' recommendation. Well aware of the problem involved, the church selected seven men from among the Greek-speaking believers, who had brought the complaint in the first place. Six of the men were evidently Jews with Greek names, but Nicolas is described as "a proselyte of Antioch." In other words, he was a Greek who had become a Jew sometime before he became a Christian. Some or all of these men may have been in that multitude on Pentecost who heard the gospel preached each in his own tongue. At least they had been in the church long enough to impress all the people with their fitness for this new service. Although we never hear of five of them again, we can assume that all seven justified the confidence of their fellow Christians.

Through what we call an ordination, the apostles accepted and dedicated them publicly to their work. Although this whole passage is generally accepted as recounting the choice of the first deacons, these seven men were never called that in the New Testament. In other words, they were not thought of as a new class of officials; the emphasis, instead, is upon their service. Three times in 6:1-4 Luke used words with the same Greek origin: "ministration," "served" tables, and "ministry." The Greek equivalents for these words came from *diakonos*, which Paul used for "deacon" (Phil. 1:1; 1 Tim. 3:8-12). As servants and ministers, then, these seven deacons have set an example for everyone similarly chosen for service.

The action of the church had divine approval, "and the number of the disciples multiplied greatly in Jerusalem" (RSV). In these early chapters that sounds almost like Luke's favorite refrain, but here he mentions a new and significant development. A large group of priests became Christians! This was a real triumph, for most priests were Sadducees. "This fact may help explain the determination of the authorities to enter upon a campaign of extermination of Christians" (Carver, 66).

II. Serving as a Martyr (6:8 to 8:1a)

Just because they were chosen to "serve tables" did not prevent those first deacons from doing other kinds of service in Christ's name. Indeed, they were probably chosen to administer relief because they had already demonstrated their effectiveness in other ways. Two of that group gained immortal reputation—one as a martyr and the other as a missionary—in extending their Christian service beyond their assignment. What a challenge to the modern deacon! What an invitation to adventurous living for Christ!

For so long have we been blessed with religious liberty in our country that it is hard for us to realize that even in the twentieth century men and women have died for their faith in Christ. May we never have to make the martyr's choice. But may all of us—deacons and members alike—grow in devotion and loyalty that we may be willing to risk all that we are to help make the gospel known around the world, to help make it clear to the lost in our neighborhood, and to help make it live in all our relationships with others.

1. The Charges Against Stephen (6:8-15)

In listing the deacons, Luke described Stephen as "a man full of faith and of the Holy Spirit" (ASV). Evidently he was the most outstanding man in the group, perhaps very near the apostles in the respect and admiration of the church. His ministry was like the course of a brilliant comet. It seemed to appear suddenly in full glory and then, just as quickly, to be gone. At least that's the impression we get from Luke's account; in one chapter he does "great wonders and miracles among the people," and in the next he dies while praying for his murderers.

As various Jewish groups from other countries came to Jerusalem to live, they established their own synagogues. Some may have been established by Jews from one particular country, but most of them were probably national mixtures although ultimately of Jewish ancestry. In one of these mixed synagogues, perhaps the one of which Stephen was a member, there arose keen opposition to the preaching of that deacon. Since the synagogue included Jews from Cilicia, Gamaliel's brilliant young

Saul may have been one of the defenders of the faith against Stephen. No matter who was there, none of them could "withstand the wisdom and the Spirit with which he spoke" (RSV).

To those Greek-speaking Jews this was not just another religious argument. They had been defeated in argument by a fellow Jew who made divine claims for Jesus of Nazareth and probably charged the Sanhedrin with his crucifixion. In the fight against unpleasant truth, men will use almost any method to protect their prejudices. These men, evidently of the Pharisee sect, did not make the mistake the Sadducees had made with the apostles, They planned by bribery and perjury to have the rank and file on their side.

When all the people had been thrown into a commotion, they caught Stephen and hustled him—perhaps in mob fashion—to the Sanhedrin. Before that court they brought their charges against Stephen, so much like the ones they had lodged against Jesus. The rumor had been that he had blasphemed "against Moses, and against God"—Moses first! At the trial the prosecution never even mentioned God; Moses and the Temple got all the attention. They were not as much concerned about discovering the truth of God as they were about protecting the form of their faith.

2. Stephen's Defense (7:1-53)

(1) Reviewing Hebrew History (1-50).—Before such a damaging accusation only the Spirit could prepare a man to defend himself. Stephen, too, claimed the promise of Jesus (Luke 12:11-12) and began to answer calmly the high priest's question. Stephen's speech is the longest one in Acts. It may seem to be a sort of roundabout way for a man to defend himself when on trial for his life. But even before the Sanhedrin, in whose eyes he

must have already seen the fatal verdict, Stephen was much more interested in witnessing to his Lord than he was in saving his own life. As the modern Christian reads Stephen's speech, he may wonder why the accused deacon thought it necessary to review so much familiar history. Surely those orthodox leaders of the people knew well the story of their nation. But Stephen had seen Hebrew history in a new light—the light of Jesus Christ!—and he wanted to win others to that point of view.

From the beginning of his speech Stephen's hearers may have known just the point he expected to make with it; but for average Christians of today his thesis would not be too clear until near the end of the speech. He left a lot to the imagination and application of his hearers, but the point he was trying to make all along was: "The history of Israel shows that God's purpose is often, indeed usually, missed by the people and that the people are thus constantly rejecting God's true representatives and missing redemption and deliverance" (Carver, 69).

Stephen began at the beginning of Hebrew history: Abraham's response to God's call to seek a promised land. God's promise included both a land and a people, and both were given in God's good time. Before the Chosen People could live in the Promised Land as a growing nation, the sons of the covenant (grandsons of Abraham) despised their brother Joseph and sold him into slavery. This was the first analogy that Stephen drew: The Jews had treated Jesus much like the patriarchs treated Joseph.

But God's will could not so easily be thwarted. The brothers' evil deed was turned into a blessing, and Jacob's family was saved from famine by finding refuge in Joseph's Egypt. Within three or four centuries, however, the children of Israel became slaves rather than guests of the Egyptians. Then God raised up Moses, whom

Stephen's hearers so revered, but he was rejected by their fathers, not once, but several times. This same Moses had promised: "A prophet shall the Lord your God raise up unto you of your brethren; him shall ye hear."

Furthermore, even though the Israelites had obeyed the Lord in maintaining the tabernacle in the wilderness and building the Temple in Jerusalem, they had let their devotion to a house of worship take the place of their loyalty to God, whose throne is the heaven and whose footstool is the earth. Thus did Stephen defend himself against their charges by trying to point out the weakness of the race in rejecting its deliverers and by showing the relative significance of Moses and the Temple in the purpose of God.

(2) Condemning the Sanhedrin (51-53).—The Sanhedrin understood even better than the modern reader the point that Stephen was making, and they probably were becoming restless under his calm and relentless indictment. Stephen must have sensed their mood; for instead of continuing to interpret Hebrew history, he suddenly broke forth into violent condemnation of his judges. From both his eyes and tongue flashed fire—the fire of the Spirit's empowered prophet! Although they prided themselves on being sons of the covenant in the flesh, Stephen declared that in the way they thought and felt and heard —always resisting the Holy Spirit—they had no part in that covenant. They had persecuted God's messengers of judgment. And even more heinous!—they had murdered the Just One of God. "Not he, Stephen, but they themselves were the violators of God's law!" (Smith, 54). Stephen was a deacon, but here he did the work of a prophet, declaring the truth of God even to those who did not want to hear it.

3. The First Martyr (7:54 to 8:1a)

That was all the Sanhedrin could stand. Concerning Jesus, they had heard that charge of murder once too often. But the best they could do with the truth was to try to silence it with primitive cruelty and murder. Like animals, "they gnashed on him with their teeth."

Stephen must have known then that only his blood would satisfy them, but he did not cower before them. Possessed by the Holy Spirit, he had a vision of God's glory with Jesus standing at his right hand. Above the angry muttering of the court Stephen's voice rose again, not in tones of searing accusation, but in serene exaltation as he described his sublime vision. Neither court nor crowd waited for a verdict. They had heard enough— more than enough! They stopped their ears lest they hear more. Probably dragging and beating him, they took Stephen outside their holy city to be stoned to death.

According to ancient Hebrew law, stoning was the accepted punishment for the blasphemer. But Roman law forbade the Sanhedrin to carry through a death sentence until the case had been reviewed by some Roman authority. Stephen was the victim, then, of just a mob. His words had touched off their smoldering prejudice. Thus were they fired to batter a man with heavy rocks—even while the man prayed for them!—until he died in his own blood.

How childish was that crowd in trying to silence with stones the truth of Christ! They could still the voice of only one witness, but they could not keep the Spirit from touching a hundred others. They probably gloated over Stephen's death; they did not know what the centuries would prove: "The blood of the martyrs is the seed of the church."

Indeed, who can say what effect Stephen's death had upon one young man? As a native of Tarsus in Cilicia, he may have disputed with Stephen in the synagogue of Grecian Jews (6:9). At his feet the witnesses against Stephen, who were supposed to throw the first stones, had laid their garments. But he was not just a spectator, for Saul was "consenting unto his death." (See his own confession in 22:20.)

III. SERVING AS A MISSIONARY (8:1b-40)

This is a chapter about laymen in the first Jerusalem church. Seven were chosen for special service. One of them earned immortal glory as the first Christian martyr. Another, as a missionary, was just as zealous in witnessing.

Perhaps few deacons think of themselves as missionaries. Certainly, few of them are ever appointed for service with any of our mission boards. Many of the others do not think of themselves as missionaries because their definition of the word is limited. A missionary is someone sent on a mission. "A missionary does not necessarily go outside of his country, his state, or even his own community. A true missionary needs only to go outside himself." That's all any church member needs to do to be a missionary: escape the prison of his self-consciousness and fear and declare even to his nearest neighbor the life he has found in Christ.

1. The First Persecution (1b-4)

Frequently the apostles must have recalled those last words of Jesus before his ascension. What a task he had outlined for them! In the years that immediately followed the coming of the Spirit at Pentecost, some of them probably wondered when they were supposed to take the gospel into Judea and Samaria. Whatever the true explanation, the fact remains that Acts 8:4 is Luke's first hint that the good news was being declared outside Jerusalem. And see what it took to get that expansion movement started!

On the very day that Stephen was stoned to death, a wave of persecution broke against the church in Jerusalem. Both Pharisees and Sadducees were united in their opposition to the men of the Way. Luke tells of no official decree issued against the Christians, but evidently the Jews made clear their feelings toward the believers. The stoning of Stephen would have been enough to crystallize the opposition and spur it on to find new victims.

Another factor in the success of the persecution was its discovery of a leader. The same young man, in his early thirties, who watched approvingly the stoning of Stephen now began to take a more active part in the devastation of the church. Probably with the help of many informers he went from house to house and dragged off both men and women to prison. Why the apostles did not leave the city and why they were not jailed with the rest presents a double puzzle. Certainly their courage cannot be questioned. Perhaps the persecutors thought they could take care of the twelve later after dispersing the church.

But Saul and his crowd underestimated the power and character of the gospel and the purpose of the Spirit. For the Spirit used the persecution to send witnesses into Judea and Samaria. They needed no upper room or Temple porch; they did not need the help and presence of the apostles; even as they left all these in Jerusalem, they "went about preaching the word."

2. Philip Preaches in Samaria (5-13)

Philip the deacon was one of those who left Jerusalem. Because of Luke's general statement in verse 4, we are sure that his story of Philip's witnessing is only one of many that might have been told. As a Grecian Jew Philip may have had less prejudice against Samaritans than did the Palestinian Jews. Certainly any city in Samaria should have been a good place to hide from the Pharisee heresy hunters. But Philip did not seem to be so much concerned about hiding as he was about preaching Christ. Here is another deacon becoming a principal witness to the word of God in Christ. Even unbelievers in modern America will listen to the lay preacher who knows the gospel and is able to declare it.

This was not the first time that the good news of God had been declared in Samaria; Jesus had a fruitful ministry there early in his career (John 4). Multitudes of the Samaritans heard Philip preach and saw the great miracles he performed, driving out unclean spirits, healing the palsied and lame. His works reinforced his words, and his words interpreted his works. The people rejoiced in the good things he did and said.

But another wonder worker had already won the admiration of the people. A magician named Simon had amazed the people with his tricks and had led them to believe that he was "some great one." Only a people whose mind is immature or whose religion is barren would have been taken in by such a quack. An immature mind and a barren religion are not restricted to one class of people. Even in the midst of our marvelous twentieth century many of our own neighbors are having their sincere religious longings exploited by teachers of hollow philosophies and man-centered faiths.

But it need not always be so. For a long time Simon had his way with the Samaritans, but that did not keep them from believing the "good news about the kingdom of God and the name of Jesus Christ" when the missionary deacon from Jerusalem preached to them. In that preaching they discovered satisfaction for their deep need, and they turned from Simon and acknowledged their faith in Christ by baptism. Even Simon professed his faith and was baptized. In the light of the proposition he would later make to the apostles, one wonders how sincere was his profession. Luke could only recount what Simon claimed to have happened to him.

3. The Apostles Strengthen Philip's Work (14-25)

Somehow word of Philip's success in Samaria got back to Jerusalem. Many of the disciples were pleased with the news. But others in the Jerusalem church were disturbed, for the church appointed Peter and John to visit the new Samaritan believers.

Evidently the two apostles came without prejudice; for when they saw that the Samaritans' response to the gospel was genuine, they prayed "that they might receive the Holy Spirit." Of course the Spirit had already effected salvation in their lives, and they had been baptized in the name of Jesus Christ. But Peter and John prayed that the Spirit might come upon these Samaritan believers in some unmistakable way—perhaps as at Pentecost—that he might build them up in understanding and spiritual power.

Simon the magician saw all that the apostles did and was very much impressed by the fact that the Spirit's power was manifest in the behavior or words of those on whom the apostles laid their hands. It is hardly possible that the apostles had laid their hands on Simon, for a Spirit-empowered man would never have made the proposition he put before the apostles. Indeed, his proposition raises the question about the sincerity of his profession of faith. It revealed a twofold misinterpretation of the Spirit: first, he thought he could buy the power of the Spirit; second, he wanted to *use* that power instead of waiting to be used by it. Simon was still the magician!

Spineless folk may criticize Peter's reply as unkind. But that was no time for a mild rebuke. This Simon was no simpleton; he was dreaming of the profitable use he could make of that wondrous power. In strong and blunt language Peter reprimanded him. That it was not a curse on Simon is shown by Peter's suggestion in verse 22. But what a fearful warning. We don't know what became of Simon. There is fear and regret but no real repentance in his final appeal to Peter. But he has left his name—simony—for the repulsive practice of trying to buy honors or office in the church.

Surely the experience with Simon increased the apostles' prestige and led the Samaritans to take with even greater seriousness their new allegiance to Christ. Peter and John stayed with them for a while to help them understand more fully the Christian witness and the message of the Lord. Then encouraged by the Spirit's confirmation of that new missionary advance, they "evangelized many villages of the Samaritans" (Carver, 85) on their way back to Jerusalem.

4. Philip Wins the Ethiopian (26-40)

Thus it was a Grecian deacon who, following the martyrdom of another Grecian deacon, was used of the Spirit to declare the gospel of grace to the hated Samaritans. Neither the creed nor race of needy men were barriers for his missionary zeal. Soon the Spirit called him on another mission which would make him an example to the rest of the world in declaring the gospel to men of different skin coloring.

An angel of the Lord instructed Philip to leave Samaria and go south on the road from Jerusalem to Gaza. As he walked along the road, he began slowly to overtake a handsome chariot. Responding to the Spirit's suggestion, Philip ran up to the chariot. Perhaps he paused as he came up behind it; at least he had time to hear its occupant reading and to recognize the passage as from Isaiah the prophet. Probably in subsequent conversation Philip discovered the identity of the earnest reader. He was a gentleman of authority from the court of Candace (a title rather than a name), queen of Ethiopia, the country south of Egypt. He was also a Jewish proselyte. As he returned from a worship pilgrimage to Jerusalem, he read from the roll of Isaiah, perhaps just purchased on this trip.

Recognizing the passage which the eunuch was reading and perhaps sensing some bewilderment in his voice, Philip asked, "Understandest thou what thou readest?" What a humble and teachable spirit the Ethiopian revealed in his reply! He was reading from Isaiah 53, and he asked the question we might ask had we never heard of Jesus Christ. Isaiah's picture of the Suffering Servant does not make easy reading for those who never heard of the crucified One. But it was just the text that Philip needed to declare the atonement which Jesus had made on the cross. It was just the text he needed to paint a picture of the world's sin mirrored in the life of every sinner. It was all the text he needed to lead a man who already believed in God to find a saving faith in Jesus Christ. "Then Philip opened his mouth, and beginning with this scripture he told him the good news of Jesus" (RSV).

So well did the Spirit work through Philip that when the chariot came near a pool or stream of water, the Ethiopian asked whether he might be baptized. Philip may have questioned him as to his faith, and the man may have replied with some simple confession, but the best manuscripts do not include verse 37. It was evidently added to include a confession formula considered important as church life became more formal and liturgical. "The New Testament provides no form of words for receiving confessions of faith and any such form is foreign to the spirit of Christianity" (Carver, 88). More significant is the fact that Luke emphasizes this as real baptism, not only in form but in meaning.

After Philip had been caught away by the Spirit, the eunuch "went on his way rejoicing." Through him the gospel was carried to another continent. Philip meanwhile continued his preaching mission to Azotus and northward along the coast to Caesarea. About twenty years later Paul would visit with him and his family there (Acts 21:8-10).

Chosen for service to needy Christians, Stephen and Philip, two of the seven whom we now call deacons, set patterns in martyrdom and evangelism for every modern deacon and believer. They were zealous in witnessing.

For Review and Further Study

1. List two or three problems of the New Testament church that Luke mentions in Acts.
2. What were the qualifications for the first deacons? How do they compare with standards for deacons in your church?
3. On what charges was Stephen tried by the Sanhedrin?
4. What was the theme of Stephen's defense before the court?
5. Did Stephen die by court action or mob violence? Explain your answer. What were some results of his martyrdom?
6. Who is a missionary?
7. How did Philip obey Christ's commission? How successful was he among the people hated by orthodox Jews?
8. What does "simony" mean? Tell the story behind the word.
9. In what act did the Ethiopian symbolize his experience of faith?

OBEDIENT TO DIVINE DIRECTION

Acts 9:1 to 12:23

I. *Surrender to Christ* (9:1-30)

    1. The Conversion of Saul (1-9)
    2. Ananias Speaks for the Lord (10-19*a*)
    3. Saul Begins His Ministry (19*b*-30)

II. *Adventure in the Spirit* (9:31 to 11:18)

    1. Peter Heals Aeneas and Raises Dorcas (9:31-43)
    2. The Visions of Two Men (10:1-16)
    3. Jew Meets Gentile in Christ's Name (10:17-33)
    4. The Spirit Enlightens and Endues (10:34-48)
    5. Peter Answers Charges of the Church (11:1-18)

III. *Teach for the Kingdom* (11:19-30)

    1. A Thriving Mission Station (19-24)
    2. Barnabas Enlists Saul as Helper (25-30)

IV. *Wait on the Lord* (12:1-23)

    1. Peter Is Delivered from Prison (1-17)
    2. Herod Is Judged in Death (18-23)

OBEDIENT TO DIVINE DIRECTION

Acts 9:1 to 12:23

Those first-century Christians were committed to Christ and possessed by the Spirit. Why should we wonder, then, at the reality of their fellowship or their zeal in witnessing? Could such marveling reveal our own unacknowledged weakness and inadequacy? Of course that Jerusalem church was nearer the first Pentecost than we are; and because some among them had known Jesus in the flesh, they had blessings that we do not know. On the other hand, we have the New Testament and nineteen centuries of assurance that the gospel can meet victoriously any opposition. We can marvel all we like at the character and work of the Jerusalem church. But the Lord prefers our work to our wonder, our allegiance to our amazement.

Another characteristic of those first-century Christians was their obedience to divine direction. Of course the events recounted in Acts 9-12 were not the only instances of that obedience; it began with their waiting in Jerusalem for power. But in this section we find three church leaders who set a wonderful example—for their day and ours!—in hearing and obeying the Lord's command.

I. Surrender to Christ (9:1-30)

Surrender—that's the first step in obedience, isn't it? He who would obey another must give up some of his rights in a certain area. Thus the citizen is obedient to

[handwritten margin notes: Saul. Key man— God put his finger on Paul at right time struck down— Judgment swift Face to face with Jesus. Face conscience Pushed to christianity what he did to christ men speechless Blindness gave him of the remedy theology]

traffic regulations, the farmer to the laws of nature, the fullback to the rules of the game. And everybody is obedient to something; everyone surrenders all or part of his life to some person or force. Then the fact of surrender is relatively unimportant. But the significance of life itself is determined by the character of the person or idea to whom one surrenders.

Saul the persecuting Pharisee made that discovery on the road to Damascus. He surrendered to Christ. To live forever the eternal kind of life every person must make that same surrender. Thus in this chapter we are brought back to consider the beginning of Christian experience.

1. The Conversion of Saul (1-9)

Our first acquaintance with Saul came at the stoning of Stephen (7:58). He it was who watched the clothes of those who killed that noble deacon. But we notice that he was no mere spectator; indeed he became the leader of the first persecution of Christians (8:3). So furiously burned his zeal for the orthodox faith against "those of the Way" that he became a fiery scourge, driving most of the Christians out of Jerusalem, imprisoning some, and probably making some others renounce their faith in Christ.

Had Saul continued to persecute the Christians, we might never have heard of him. His name, if preserved at all, would have been just one among many who have tried to obstruct the will of God. But because of what happened on the Damascus road and because of his loyalty to his new-found Lord, his name is known around the world, and his inspired words continue to bless believers.

Before we examine his conversion experience, let us review briefly some facts about the man himself. Born in Tarsus, a prominent city in the province of Cilicia in

Asia Minor, Saul had the advantages of a well-to-do and orthodox Jewish home, plus the contacts with Greek and Roman culture in a seaport and university center. When he was about thirteen years of age, he was sent to Jerusalem for further study under Gamaliel, the leading teacher of the Pharisees, the sect whose view of the law Saul and his family shared. His speeches and letters of maturity show how broad yet thorough was his education: speech facility in three languages (Aramaic, Greek, Latin), full and accurate knowledge of the Old Testament, easy familiarity with the basic problems of pagan theology and philosophy, keen logical powers, remarkable literary skill. There was never any question about his loyalty to the Jewish faith (26:4-5).

It was that blind loyalty that spurred him from house to house in Jerusalem seeking Christians for punishment. Just when he thought he had completed his work in Jerusalem, disturbing reports began to come in from other regions and cities. Armed with letters of authority from the high priest, Saul set out with some companions for Damascus.

To get the full story of the great event that happened on that trip, we need to put 22:6-11 and 26:12-18 alongside this passage. In them Saul himself describes his conversion. Saul and his companions had almost completed their 150-mile journey when suddenly at midday a light, brighter than the sun, burst upon them. Saul was stunned by its brilliance and fell to the ground. Then he heard a voice calling him and asking a question. Saul countered with another question, and its answer revealed the identity of the voice in the light: "I am Jesus, whom you are persecuting" (RSV).

Immediately there must have flashed across Saul's mind the picture of Stephen standing defenseless before the Sanhedrin's wrath and declaring in sublime ecstasy,

"Behold, I see the heavens opened, and the Son of man standing at the right hand of God" (7:56 RSV). He had seen that deacon die praying for his murderers. "Could it be," he may have wondered, "that these uneducated people have found that satisfying and contagious faith in God for which I have sought so long?" Who knows what questions were turning Saul's well-ordered, self-righteous mind into a battleground for truth? That something had been trying to undermine his self-satisfaction and cruel intolerance is revealed in Jesus' comment: "It hurts you to kick against the goads" (26:14 RSV).

Then Saul made his surrender! Thus far had he come in fanatic devotion to the Scriptures and the traditional interpretation of them. But on his way to Damascus he surrendered to the living word of God. Thus far had he come in eager loyalty to narrow, exclusive Judaism. But on his way to arrest some who had acknowledged their faith in Jesus Christ, Saul turned himself over to that same Master. Of course he continued into Damascus, but Saul made an about face that day which became the focal point of his whole Christian ministry. Surely this conversion was only the first step in his Christian experience, but without a first step there cannot be a second or a third.

The Lord always has an answer when the surrendered soul says, "Lord, what wilt thou have me to do?" He told Saul to go on into the city for further instructions. Obeying, Saul discovered his blindness, and the leader had to be led. Meanwhile his companions had seen the light and heard the voice, but they did not understand the Hebrew speech.

2. Ananias Speaks for the Lord (10-19a)

Saul was taken to the home of a man named Judas, very likely an orthodox Jewish leader. For three days he would neither eat nor drink but sat alone in his strange new world of blindness and sought God's strength through prayer. Then the Lord gave him a vision of the one who would be used to restore his sight. But that one, named Ananias, was not enthusiastic about his assignment. The Jewish believers in Damascus had heard about Saul's havoc among the Christians in Jerusalem, and Ananias knew his errand in Damascus. But his fears were stilled by the Lord's assurance. Whether he understood the significance of the commission he had for Saul from the Lord we do not know, but Ananias obeyed the Lord.

What a greeting he gave that persecutor! Despite the things he had heard about this brilliant but intolerant young Pharisee, Ananias was led by God's grace to say, "Brother Saul"! How wonderful those words must have sounded to the blind man! Then Ananias identified the roadside visitant and announced his own purpose. Immediately Saul received his sight, and Ananias delivered the Lord's message to his newest convert: "You will be a witness for him [God] to all men" 22:15 RSV).

Nothing else is known about Ananias. But what else need we know to learn a great lesson from him? God used "this timid, obscure man to lead the mighty persecutor into apostleship. This was a good experience for both men, and a good lesson for disciples of Jesus in all times" (Carver, 95). Many Christians will never be great soul-winners—great, that is, in terms of numbers. But God doesn't measure greatness that way. Who could say who is the greater in his sight: Dwight L. Moody, who won thousands to Christ, or the earnest Sunday school teacher who won Dwight L. Moody? George W. Truett or the young evangelist who brought him to the hour of decision? Your pastor or that Sunday school teacher who works quietly but persistently to win two Intermediate boys? Great disciples of the Master are in the making, but at least one of them may never serve unless *you* win him to the Saviour.

3. Saul Begins His Ministry (19b-30)

What a change Christ can make in a man! He made a preacher out of a persecutor! Both Christians and Jews were astonished at Saul's words. They had heard of his work in Jerusalem, and they knew his reason for coming to Damascus. Doubtless the Christians were as surprised as the Jews at the change that had taken place in him. Their relief may have been mixed with suspicion until they heard the story that Ananias must have told his fellow believers. While the Christians began to feel strengthened by their new recruit, the Jews were confused by his powerful new message that Jesus is the Christ.

In Galatians 1:15-18 Saul explained the meaning of Luke's "many days" in Acts 9:23. Although he was successful in his debate with the Jews, Saul must have felt the need for more study of the Scriptures and for sustained reflection upon their meaning in the light of his new-found faith in Christ. The Lord had dealt directly with him; Saul must have felt that he ought to deal directly with the Lord instead of seeking guidance from the apostles in Jerusalem. Even after about three years in Arabia he still returned to Damascus rather than to Jerusalem.

Whatever reception Saul may have expected in Jerusalem, it could have been no worse than that which awaited him at Damascus. Just as the Grecian Jews in Jerusalem had sought Stephen's life when he bested them in debate, the Damascus Jews "took counsel to kill" Saul. The former persecutor then began to drink from the cup which he had filled for others. He who had come arrogantly to Damascus escaped over its wall like a hunted criminal.

Back in Jerusalem Saul tried to identify himself with the believers there, but they were suspicious of him, fearing some trick and betrayal. They still remembered his "threatenings and slaughter" of three years before. They had probably heard of his conversion, but what had he done to prove its reality? Only one man of influence seemed to be moved by Saul's story and vouched for his sincerity before the apostles.

Saul turned to good account the two weeks he spent as guest of Peter, preaching Christ and debating with the Grecian Jews. Although the persecution of the Christians may have lagged after Saul's conversion, the animosity of the Jews still smoldered. Saul's testimony blew it into flame. Both the message and the messenger enraged them. Had he not been the darling of orthodoxy, the sword of the Sanhedrin! To have this man declare Christ as Lord made them writhe and howl for his life. Then the Christians realized what they had on their hands, and probably hoping that the Lord could use him more effectively elsewhere, they helped Saul get away to Tarsus. In 22:17-21 Paul gives another reason for his leaving Jerusalem.

II. ADVENTURE IN THE SPIRIT (9:31 to 11:18)

Christ's offer of salvation is not for safety's sake alone. Every Christian is saved to serve. Unless he gives a reasonably consistent testimony to Christ's work in his own life and demonstrates a vital faith by the way he lives, both Christians and non-Christians have a right to question the reality of that man's professed trust in Christ as Saviour and allegiance to him as Lord. The service to which Christians are called is never humdrum or routine. Of course it must be rendered daily, and in big and little ways. But the true Christian witness is an ever fresh and often dangerous adventure. Until the end of the age the world will oppose the gospel of Christ. Declaring that gospel in its fullest meaning, therefore, will always be a great adventure—an adventure in following the Spirit!

1. Peter Heals Aeneas and Raises Dorcas (9:31-43)

So long as the church was centered in Jerusalem, Luke had few problems in telling his story. But as Christian communities began to develop in various communities of Judea, Galilee, and Samaria, he found it difficult to tell of so many things that were happening simultaneously. Instead of trying to follow Saul to Tarsus, he let his narrative pick up the work of Peter for a while. But the work of apostles, deacons, and all the disciples was reflected in the report that the church was made larger as it walked "in the fear of the Lord and in the comfort of the Holy Spirit."

Peter had already preached in Samaria (8:25), but here he seems to have been on a preaching tour by himself as he visited the saints (believers, dedicated ones) in Lydda. There by means of a miracle of healing he caused many to turn to the Lord. For eight years Aeneas had been the bedridden victim of some kind of paralysis; we assume that he was a Christian. To him Peter gave a healing command something like this: "Jesus Christ heals you here and now; stand and make up your bed."

News of that miracle and of Peter's presence in Lydda spread to Joppa, about twelve miles away. Believers there thought of him immediately when they suffered a great loss. Dorcas had earned the love and appreciation of the whole church through the "good works and acts of charity" (RSV) which she was always doing. When Peter arrived in Joppa, the believers took him to the upper room where the body had been laid, and there a crowd of mourning widows began to show him the things Dorcas had made for them. Their grief was exceeded only by their gratitude.

Peter did not at once attempt to exercise the power that he knew was available. Instead, he kneeled and prayed to know the will of God and to have himself prepared as the channel of God's power. Of course the saints and widows marveled and rejoiced when he presented the living Dorcas. But the greater fruit of the deed came when "many believed in the Lord" because of it. After such an ingathering, what else could Peter do but continue to witness and to teach?

What an adventure his short trip had been already! The Spirit had led him and empowered him to heal the sick and restore the dead. What more remarkable things could happen to him?

2. The Visions of Two Men (10:1-16)

A Roman centurion named Cornelius was stationed at Caesarea, just thirty miles north of Joppa. His company was a part of an Italian regiment. But Cornelius, though loyal to Rome, had forsaken Roman paganism; he was not a Jewish proselyte according to the law, but he reverenced God, prayed to him constantly, and was liberal in his charity to the people.

About three o'clock one afternoon (a Jewish hour of prayer) he was thoroughly frightened by the sudden appearance of a heavenly messenger before him. When Cornelius had acknowledged his presence, the angel told him that "his prayers and his alms proved his sincerity and won the ear of God" (Robertson, 134). When the angel had disappeared, Cornelius charged two trusted servants and a devout soldier with the errand to Joppa.

That was the first vision—a message of God to a Gentile.

Next day in Joppa while the noon meal was being prepared in the house of Simon the tanner, Peter went up to the rooftop to pray. While he prayed, the very hungry apostle lost himself in a trance and saw a strange sight in the sky. A great cloth seemed to be let down from heaven to the earth, and "in it were all kinds of animals and reptiles and wild birds" (RSV). While Peter stared, he heard a voice inviting him to kill and eat. But he wasn't *that* hungry! According to the Jewish law some of those animals were unclean, and even those that were acceptable had been defiled by contact with the others. No, Peter wasn't that hungry, and he told the Lord so in no uncertain terms: "By no means, Lord, for I never did eat anything common and unclean" (Carver, 1C8). Three times he gave that answer to the same invitation, and three times he was rebuked: "What God hath cleansed, you must not call common" (RSV).

3. Jew Meets Gentile in Christ's Name (10:17-33)

Of course Peter was perplexed (better than "doubted" as in KJV) by the vision; he was at a loss to know what it meant. But he didn't have long to wonder, for the Spirit told him that three men were looking for him and that he should go with them without hesitation. Peter had them spend the night in Simon's house, and during that night and the trip on the next day Peter began to see the meaning of his vision. Of course it was not unusual that a Jew have a heavenly visitant, but when had God begun to reveal his will to Gentiles in that way? If God considered a Gentile worthy of such a boon, could

they really be common in his sight? The vision on the
housetop began to make sense.

Meanwhile, Cornelius had called together his kinsmen and intimate friends to welcome and hear the heaven-sent guest. When the company of men (Peter had
brought six companions) arrived at the entrance of the
centurion's home, Cornelius prostrated himself before
Peter and did him reverence (preferable to "worshiped").
But Peter was embarrassed by such a demonstration.
Then talking together, the Jew and the Gentile entered a
large room where a small congregation was waiting to hear Peter preach the gospel. He reminded them
that he was a Jew and that a Jew could not be really
friendly with a Gentile. "There was nothing in the
Mosaic law at all so rigid as Peter's rule here, but the
strict Jews did seek to apply this exclusive regulation"
(Carver, 111). But in spite of the rule, God had shown
him that he should not call any man common. How
quickly the vision had come clear and taken effect! Would
God that all his children might learn the same lesson!

When Peter asked why he had been sent for, Cornelius
recounted his own vision and prepared the way for Peter
to declare the full gospel. What an adventure the Spirit
had opened unto Peter! Before him was an "eager, rev-
erent, expectant audience, the first company of Gentiles to
hear the gospel, and by their own invitation" (Carver,
112).

4. The Spirit Enlightens and Endues (10:34-48)

Peter's first sentence was tremendous evidence that
the Spirit had enlightened at least one man. Of course,
God's impartiality toward men had been taught in the
Old Testament, but the strict Jews of the first century
had almost forgotten that in their zeal for separation.
By "acceptable" he did not mean, of course, that the

God-fearers in other nations had been saved. Rather, they were worthy to hear and respond to the message of Christ. The Gentile need not become a Jew before becoming a Christian.

Having settled that point, Peter launched into his sermon. Certainly he only hinted at the purpose ("preaching good news of peace" RSV) and ministry ("went about doing good") of Jesus. The Gentiles had heard these things, but Peter said, "We are witnesses of all things which he did"—of his crucifixion, his resurrection, and his commission. "This first message of Peter to the Gentiles corresponds in broad outline with Mark's Gospel. Mark heard Peter preach many times and evidently planned his Gospel (the Roman Gospel) on this model" (Robertson, 144-145). Of course the theme of the sermon was Jesus of Nazareth whom God—already reverenced by Cornelius—ordained to be the "Judge of the living and the dead" (ASV).

Peter had practically given his invitation when suddenly "the Holy Spirit fell on all them that heard the word" (ASV). Before they made a public profession of their faith, they believed in their hearts; and the Holy Spirit proved their faith by enduing them as he had the disciples on Pentecost. Of course the Jewish Christians were amazed at the positive evidence of the Spirit's coming upon Gentile believers. There was no reason to delay their baptism since it was only a symbol of what had already happened to them in the Spirit.

5. Peter Answers Charges of the Church (11:1-18)

But still another adventure awaited Peter in Jerusalem, for there he was called upon to explain his evangelistic work among the Gentiles. Imagine that! Of course the whole church at Jerusalem did not ask for an explanation; many had probably rejoiced in the news from

Caesarea. But one party—"they that were of the circumcision"—was displeased and flung at Peter its charge of disloyalty to the Jewish faith.

It is hard for us to understand their position. They were Christians, but they were also Jews, and they looked upon Christianity as being but an extension of the Jewish faith. For so long had they been loyal to the rabbinical interpretation of the laws of Moses that they couldn't appreciate the freedom which should have been theirs through Christ Jesus. In their sight, the gospel was for Jews only, and until a man had become a Jew, he could not become a follower of Jesus. Here is the first instance of the Judaizers' influence, but in a short time it would lead to bitter controversy among first-century Christians.

Answering their charge, Peter reviewed all that happened to him and all that he had done. He made sure they understood that the vision on the rooftop in Joppa had been a divine presentation; he also emphasized his orthodox reply to the invitation to eat unclean meat. Then he pointed out the six brethren ("of the circumcision" 10:45) who had accompanied him into the house of the Gentile. Peter knew that he had been invited to tell the centurion and his household how they might be saved. Then had come the Spirit in power upon them before he could finish speaking. And Peter closed his defense with a question: "If then God gave the same gift to them as he gave to us when we believed in the Lord Jesus Christ, who was I that I could withstand God?" (RSV).

To that question the party of the circumcision had no answer—at least not for the time being. Glorifying God they acknowledged his gift of salvation to the Gentiles. But the tense of the verb may suggest some reluctance on their part. In other words they seem to have acknowledged this instance but not to have committed themselves

to the established principle of allowing Gentiles freely
to become Christians.

III. TEACH FOR THE KINGDOM (11:19-30)

Obedience to divine direction begins with surrender
to Christ and continues in a Spirit-led adventure in Christian living. Much of that living is not dramatic but
involves routine responsibilities in more or less insig-
nificant places. The visiting evangelist may seem to live
an exciting life of unending victories over the forces of
evil. Fruits of his testimony are usually striking and
immediate. But who does the spade work? Through the
years of their childhood, who help boys and girls face
the claims of Christ? Who lead the new converts to
grow in Bible knowledge and church loyalty? Whether
parents, counselors, or sponsors, they are all *teachers*.

If we would be obedient to divine direction, we must
teach for the kingdom—teach the lost, teach the saved,
teach the Word.

1. A Thriving Mission Station (19-24)

Already we have reviewed some of the remarkable
things that happened during the persecution that followed Stephen's stoning. While Philip was at work in
Samaria, other disciples went even farther away from
home, "preaching the word to none but unto the Jews
only."

Of course many who fled Jerusalem during the persecution were Grecian Jews, and some of them went to Antioch. There in the capital of Syria and the third most
important city in the Roman Empire they found Syrians,
Greeks, Latins, and Jews. Evidently more liberal than
Palestinian Jews in their appreciation of Gentiles, some
Jewish Christians who were natives of Cyprus and

Cyrene began to preach to Greeks in Antioch. (The manuscripts are divided on whether this should be Greeks or Grecian Jews, but the sense of the story favors the former.) Thus about the same time that Peter visited Cornelius, some Gentiles in Antioch were giving a hearty response to the gospel.

As on other occasions the church in Jerusalem sent a representative to investigate the report from Antioch. How fortunate that they selected Barnabas! Certainly they must have had full confidence in him and wanted him to help the new believers. He was enthusiastic over what he found, and he began to give a good account of the meaning of his name (see 4:36). His ministry among them was most fruitful. Under lay leadership this new mission station had attracted the attention of the apostles in Jerusalem. But by the foresight of Barnabas and the power of the Spirit it rapidly became a center of Christian witnessing.

What a fine tribute Luke paid Barnabas! As Luke, the author of Acts, looked back upon the way the controversy with the Judaizers grew, and as he recalled what Barnabas had meant to Saul in getting him started in his great ministry, he recognized some qualities in the man which must have helped the growth of that new Antioch church. No nobler tribute could any church worker desire: "He was a good man, and full of the Holy Spirit and of faith" (ASV).

2. Barnabas Enlists Saul as Helper (25-30)

Seeing how the Lord was blessing the work among the Greeks and remembering the remarkable qualities of Saul, whom he had endorsed before the apostles, Barnabas set out to Tarsus for help. Although Luke does not tell us what Saul had been doing since returning to his home town, the apostle himself later claimed that the churches in Judea rejoiced because of his preaching in Syria and Cilicia (Gal. 1:21-24). In him Barnabas saw just the man to do a great work among both believing and unbelieving Greeks. Thus Barnabas became the instrument of the Lord in setting Saul on the way toward fulfilling his original commission.

For a whole year Barnabas and Saul worked together with that Antioch church. Certainly they must have preached; surely they did their share of soul-winning; but Luke mentions neither ministry. Instead, he says, "They assembled themselves with the church, and taught much people." And what teaching it must have been! For it bore fruit in two very real ways.

First, the disciples (learners) "were called Christians first in Antioch." Probably it was first used in derision, but the title was accepted by the disciples as a mark of honor. The Greek word for "were called" suggests being named after one's business. "It is pleasing to find that the name was first given because working in the Christ way seemed to outsiders to be the business of 'the disciples'" (Carver, 125). Barnabas and Saul taught them well that their lives should be distinctive from their non-Christian neighbors.

Second, when a prophet from Jerusalem foretold a worldwide famine, these Greek Christians determined to send relief to their brethren in Judea. They may have known or suspected how one element in the Jerusalem church felt about them, but that did not affect their practice of Christian love when they thought the others might be in need. They paid back suspicion with generosity. With their substance they demonstrated the reality of Christian fellowship.

Yes, these Greek Christians were well taught by Barnabas and Saul. Without that kind of teaching, the work at Antioch might never have grown into a church

—a church of active Christian living, of broad generosity, of missionary zeal. Teaching in the Spirit for the kingdom is still the secret of the great church, whether large or small.

IV. WAIT ON THE LORD (12:1-23)

This may be the most difficult assignment a Christian can have in being obedient to divine direction. But at times that is all that one can do. The disciples found it so in the ten days before Pentecost. But their waiting was not mere idling; it was a continuation of their fellowship with God in prayer. That kind of waiting is never wasted. Sometimes we must wait on the Lord because of evil forces about us. Man thinks in years; but God in centuries and millenniums. The earnest Christian who does not see and hope beyond the years can easily become discouraged by the temporary triumphs of wickedness. Of course he must never relax his efforts or give up a single crusade; but while he works and prays, he must wait on the Lord.

1. Peter Is Delivered from Prison (1-17)

Up to this time (about A.D. 43 or 44) the Roman government had paid no attention to the Christians or the Jewish resentment against them. But Herod Agrippa I had good reason to use them as scapegoats in his overtures to the ruling class of Jews. Grandson of Herod the Great, ruler of Judea when Jesus was born, this Herod had been brought up in Rome. As the friend of Caligula he had been made ruler over most of Palestine. Then under Claudius he became king of the whole country, A.D. 41-44. Although he had little concern for the Jewish faith while reveling in Rome, Herod (a half Jew) became quite zealous in Palestine. James was his first victim, the first apostle to become a martyr.

But when he arrested Peter, evidently intending to kill him also, he realized that the Passover (not Easter as in KJV) was at hand. And of course the orthodox ruler would not want to spoil the feast with shed blood. For the time being, then, he put him under a four-man guard which was changed every six hours. Throughout his imprisonment the church prayed ceaselessly for him. Then on the very night before his execution Peter was awakened by an angel standing over him. The angel roused him, and when Peter stood up, his chains fell off. Then he followed the angel as if in a dream past the various guards and through the outer gate into the city.

Suddenly Peter was alone, and he stopped for a moment to make sure that it was true—the Lord had delivered him! Then he walked rapidly to the home of Mary, mother of John Mark, where he probably expected to find a good company of the church. Surely the disciples had prayed in faith, but they were not ready for so prompt an answer. "You are crazy," they told Rhoda, who declared that Peter was outside. But while they were talking, they heard Peter still knocking, and they were amazed to find him at the door. When he could get them quiet, Peter told how the Lord had delivered him.

Realizing his own personal danger and the possible danger to the believers if he should be found with them, Peter probably left Jerusalem. Surely a man who had been delivered from prison and possibly death would know how to wait until the squall of persecution had blown over.

2. Herod Is Judged in Death (18-23)

Herod's days were numbered. After he was foiled in his attempt upon Peter's life and had executed the guards, he left Jerusalem for Caesarea, the official capital. Soon after his arrival there some representatives from Phenicia, worried over the strained relations between Herod and their cities, approached one of his trusted ministers to secure an audience for them. Upon the appointed day Herod in royal regalia made a speech to the people. Josephus, a Jewish historian of that time, says that Herod appeared in a robe of silver cloth. That may account the more realistically for the people's excited flattery: "It is the voice of a god, and not of a man." They were not saying that Herod was God but that he was worthy the reverence they were already giving the Emperor. But even that was blasphemy; and when Herod accepted it, God's judgment fell quickly. And what a horribly repulsive death!

Peter and his fellow Christians had waited on the Lord. They had not stopped their work, nor had they lost heart. So great was their commission that they knew the Lord would not allow one little king forever to thwart his purpose.

FOR REVIEW AND FURTHER STUDY

1. In what four ways does this chapter describe early Christians as being obedient to divine direction?
2. List five facts of Saul's life up to the time of his conversion.
3. Tell briefly the story of Saul's conversion. In what three chapters of Acts do we find it recounted?
4. In what ways did Saul set an example for new Christians by the things he did in the years just after his conversion?
5. How did Peter explain his actions before the Jerusalem church? How do we know the Judaizers were not finally convinced?
6. List several characteristics of Barnabas.
7. What evidence do we have that the teaching of Barnabas and Saul at Antioch was successful?

V

READY TO SHARE AND DEFEND THE GOSPEL

Acts 12:24 to 15:31

I. *By Sending Out Missionaries* (12:24 to 13:3)

II. *By Preaching Fearlessly to All* (13:4 to 14:28)

    1. First Stops on Paul's First Tour (13:4-13)
    2. A Missionary's Sermon (13:14-41)
    3. From Jews to Gentiles (13:42-48)
    4. Persistent Opposition (13:49 to 14:6)
    5. Honored Then Stoned in Lystra (14:7-20)
    6. Back to Antioch (14:21-28)

III. *By Holding Fast the Simple Gospel* (15:1-31)

    1. A Dispute with the Judaizers (1-5)
    2. Discussing the Problem Openly (6-21)
    3. They Reach a Great Decision (22-31)

READY TO SHARE AND DEFEND THE GOSPEL

Acts 12:24 to 15:31

A man is expected to love his family but not to share that kind of love with the rest of the world; he cannot love other families in the same way or to the same degree that he loves his own. On the other hand, unless the Christian's love for Christ issues in love and concern for those who do not know him, we suspect either the sincerity or the maturity of that Christian's love. Unless a Christian's gratitude for his own salvation turns enthusiastically to help another receive the same gift, we wonder about the reality or depth of his experience. The gospel must be shared, and if it accomplishes its ultimate purpose in the life of a person, it *will* be shared.

Every Christian has his own way of sharing the gospel, depending upon his abilities and opportunities. But none of the so-called modern techniques can equal the effectiveness of the basic method of first-century Christians: a person-to-person witness backed by consistent Christian living.

I. By Sending Out Missionaries (12:24 to 13:3)

We usually think of those early Christians as always being ready to share the gospel, but already in our study we have discovered that one group in the Jerusalem church seriously questioned Peter's preaching to the Gentiles. The whole church was prepared to declare the gospel, but they were not all ready to share it. In this chapter we learn of a church of both Gentile and Jewish Christians who *were* ready to share the gospel and proved their readiness by sending out missionaries.

While the disciples waited on the Lord and Herod was judged in death, the Lord was at work in the lives of men. A persecutor might rise and fall, but "the Word of the Lord went on increasing and being multiplied" (Carver, 134). To pick up his narrative of Barnabas and Saul from 11:30, Luke told of their return to Antioch, taking with them Barnabas' cousin, John Mark.

Realizing the significance of Antioch both in his story and in the spread of Christianity, Luke took occasion to list some of the leaders of that church. Whether he intended to distinguish between prophets and teachers, we cannot say. There is a slight indication in the Greek that the first three were considered prophets and the last two teachers. Certainly their work was quite similar. These five Jewish Christians had proved their loyalty to Christ and their concern for his expanding kingdom.

Made up so largely of Greek Christians and situated on the edge of the unevangelized Empire, we can imagine that the Antioch church had often discussed its responsibility for proclaiming the gospel in the regions beyond. If Barnabas had written the history of that church, he would have mentioned many members who were concerned about brothers or cousins in Cyprus, Asia, and Greece. Whatever the burden of their prayers as they worshiped the Lord and fasted, the Holy Spirit found it a propitious time to ask that Barnabas and Saul be set apart for the work to which he had called them.

According to the record the church must have understood well the nature of that assignment. At least they did not ask for an explanation. Undoubtedly Saul had recounted his conversion and his commission. Responding to the Spirit's instructions, the church continued fasting and praying—for the two men and their projected witness—and symbolized by the laying on of hands the church's desire to set them apart. The Antioch Christians rejoiced in the Spirit's selection of their two best leaders.

Previous missionary efforts had been the work of individual Christians, driven in some instances by persecution to witness beyond the borders of their home communities. But here was a church sending forth its Spirit-called missionaries. Once empowered by the Spirit, the disciples had witnessed in Jerusalem; then by the mysterious ways of God they had begun to witness in Judea and Samaria. Finally, eighteen years after their commission had been given and 300 miles north of Olivet a Christian fellowship of Jews and Gentiles began to see the meaning of the rest of that commission.

II. By Preaching Fearlessly to All (13:4 to 14:28)

Some Christians were led by the Spirit to *send* missionaries; others were led by the same Spirit to *be* missionaries. But they were not the only ones who preached fearlessly to all. There would soon be other teams of missionaries; there would be churches in pagan centers whose members would stand against both Judaizers and heathen authorities.

Although the times are so different, the challenge for a worthy and universal witness has not changed from that first century to our own. Evil forces at home and abroad are still determined to destroy or to discredit the Christian witness. Both the judgment and the love of God must be preached unto them. At the same time, there are large groups within our churches who really do not believe in our evangelistic and missionary endeavors. Some believe that only "superior" people can appreciate the gospel. Others do lip service only to the power of the new birth; their real faith is in education, stricter laws, job insurance, housing projects, and so

forth. The present-day Christian, too, must be ready
to share the *whole* gospel.

1. First Stops on Paul's First Tour (13:4-13)

Luke was not contradicting himself when he wrote in
verse 3 that the church sent out Barnabas and Saul and
in verse 4 that they were sent by the Spirit. The Spirit
was working through the church. From Antioch the two
missionaries accompanied by John Mark went to Seleucia,
the port of Antioch, and sailed from there to Cyprus.
Your understanding of this first tour can be greatly enhanced by following it on a map. Trace it now with these
stopping places: Salamis and Paphos on Cyprus, Perga
in Pamphylia, Antioch in Pisidia, and Iconium, Lystra,
and Derbe in Lycaonia.

Although both missionaries were aware of their commission to preach to Gentiles, they went first to the synagogues to proclaim the good news. And so long as they
were acceptable there, what better place could they find
to begin their witnessing? For even though they had been
sent to the Gentiles, they would always yearn to win their
own people. In the synagogues would be both Jews and
God-fearing Gentiles.

From Salamis, where nothing unusual had happened,
they walked the hundred miles across the island to
Paphos. Adventure and victory awaited them in the
capital. Barnabas and Saul were probably there for
several weeks before news of their message led the proconsul to invite them to tell him of "the word of God."
Of course Sergius Paulus was a Roman, but he had evidently become dissatisfied with Roman religion and was
trying to discover some meaningful truth. Perhaps for
that purpose he had taken into his court a Jewish
magician named Bar-jesus (Hebrew) or Elymas (Greek).

When Elymas saw the proconsul responding favorably to the Christian message, he attempted to discredit both the message and messengers and thus prevent the ruler from discovering the truth. On their very first tour Barnabas and Saul found themselves opposed by vicious ignorance and superstition. Elymas had to be handled positively, and Saul was the man who could do it. With a piercing gaze he turned to the magician. In that moment the Spirit must have sharpened his tongue, and his words came like crisp chips from the woodsman's ax. And when Paul had finished his condemnation, the enemy of the truth "went about seeking some to lead him by the hand." His blindness was a temporary punishment and a fruitful testimony; for the proconsul was overwhelmed by this demonstration of God's power and "astonished at the teaching of the Lord" (RSV).

2. A Missionary's Sermon (13:14-41)

When the two missionaries left Antioch, Barnabas was recognized as the leader. His name is listed first in all references in Acts up to the Paphos incident. But thereafter Paul appears as the leader of all three missionary journeys; in practically every instance his name precedes the name of his partner. That Paphos incident seemed to be the occasion for another change: Saul became Paul. No one knows exactly why he began using the other name. Since he was both a Jew and a Roman citizen, he was probably given both names by his parents. Then while living and working among Jews, he used his Jewish name, changing to his Latin and Greek name when he began to work with Gentiles.

From Paphos Paul and his company sailed to Perga in the province of Pamphylia, but John Mark's desertion seems to have been the only thing worth recording about that stop. The missionaries went on a hundred miles through rugged territory to Antioch in Pisidia. In locating this city on a map, you will find that it seems also to be in Galatia. The Roman province of Galatia extended north and south almost all the way across Asia Minor. It was a political unit and included the ancient regions of Galatia (in the north), Pisidia, Lycaonia, and part of Phrygia (in the south). This province was the scene of the rest of Paul's tour.

Again the missionaries went first to a synagogue to worship and perhaps to preach. As strangers they were invited to say a few words of encouragement, and Paul was glad to respond. Addressing both the Jews and the God-fearing Gentiles, he moved quickly and easily into a review of the historical background of the Jewish people with which they were familiar. That was the approach that Stephen had made. And what better approach could there be for preaching to Jews and others acquainted with the record of God's revelation in the Old Testament?

In the midst of that review Paul suddenly introduced Jesus as a descendant of the great David and as Israel's Saviour. At first acclaimed by the prophet John, this Jesus had been rejected by the Jews and crucified by Pilate. But through the resurrection God confirmed him as his Son pictured in the Old Testament (Psalm 2:7; Isa. 55:3; Psalm 16:10). Thus the review of Israel's history served Paul only as an introduction for Jesus; and together they had significance for every man in the place. Through the risen Christ they might have remission of sins; through faith in him, they could be made righteous in God's sight—something that the law of Moses could not do.

Thus in this first recorded sermon of Paul we find a well-developed method based on expert knowledge of the Scriptures; we find also the germ of Paul's future teaching: the impotence of the law and the adequacy of God's grace appropriated by man's faith unto his salvation.

3. From Jews to Gentiles (13:42-48)

The rulers of the synagogue had hardly expected that kind of preaching from a visitor. He had shown his respect for the Law and Prophets, but his was certainly a new way of interpreting Hebrew history and the Word of God. As the visitors were leaving, the congregation begged them to come again with the same message on the next sabbath. (The correct translation of verse 42 may be found in the American Standard Version.) Some of the congregation even went along with Paul and Barnabas, perhaps to their lodging place. During that week the two missionaries probably talked with many who had heard them on the sabbath. We cannot imagine these two waiting to proclaim the gospel in worship services only.

By the next sabbath their fame had spread throughout the city. A great crowd of Jews, proselytes, and nonbelieving Gentiles gathered to hear the traveling evangelist. That was too much for the Jews. Whether they were jealous because of Paul's popularity or because the Gentiles were showing so much more interest in the gospel than in the message of Judaism, they turned against Paul and his preaching. Even while Paul was speaking, the rulers of the synagogue began to contradict him and revile his message. They had marveled at these men on the previous sabbath, but a week's review of the rabbinical interpretation of the Scriptures and discussion among themselves had led to a rearrangement of their prejudices.

Paul and Barnabas had no choice but to leave the synagogue, but first they struck out as boldly at Jewish narrowness as they had against the vicious sorcerer in

Paphos. For many reasons the missionaries had gone first to the Jews, and for nearly twenty years the Jews had received the gospel enthusiastically. But when it was presented to Jews and Gentiles on the same basis, the Jews began to reject it. Paul and Barnabas' startling announcement concerned Antioch only. They had already turned to the Gentiles before starting on their journey; they would appeal to Jews whenever they had the opportunity. Of course the Gentiles rejoiced in his declaration, and many of them believed. From Antioch and by Gentile testimony the word of the Lord for several months perhaps was spread throughout the region.

4. Persistent Opposition (13:49 to 14:6)

The Jews weren't satisfied, however, to rid their synagogue of these heretics; they must be driven out of town before they did more "damage." To accomplish that end, they asked some of the leading women of the community who were Jewish proselytes (and some of these may have been wives of city officials) to help them stir up a persecution against Paul and Barnabas. Even though the missionaries were forced to flee from Antioch, the Gentile disciples there demonstrated in some obvious way that the Holy Spirit had come upon them. That must have encouraged greatly the missionaries as they went on to Iconium.

Paul and Barnabas probably traveled the famous Roman military highway that stretched eastward nearly ninety miles to Iconium, a city of about the same size and character as Antioch. Again they went to the Jewish synagogue, but this time many believed, both Jews and Greeks. Just when they thought that their experience would be different from that in Antioch, the unbelieving (or disobedient) Jews "stirred up the Gentiles and poisoned their minds against the brethren" (RSV). Meanwhile the Christian witness evidently bore fruit. At least, the presence of the missionaries became a controversial issue in the city, and the population was divided.

Then one day Paul and Barnabas learned of a plot made by both Gentiles and Jews to attack and stone them. Neither was afraid of physical harm, but they could see no advantage in becoming the victims of a mob. Instead, they sought the same Roman road which turned southward at Iconium toward Lystra.

5. Honored Then Stoned in Lystra (14:7-20)

Since no synagogue is mentioned in Lystra and since the only opposition to the gospel was aroused by Jews from Antioch and Iconium, we may assume that Paul worked wholly with Gentiles there. One day as he was preaching with Barnabas standing by, he noticed a cripple sitting on the edge of the crowd and listening attentively to him. Paul saw faith shining through those eyes. Suddenly he stopped preaching, faced the cripple, and in a loud voice commanded him to stand up. Doubtless the crowd was stunned by the interruption, but they were not at all prepared for what happened. Perhaps still staring at Paul, the cripple leaped to his feet and began walking around. The crowd gasped and in their next breath explained the miracle in their own language and according to their own religion.

Then it was the missionaries' turn to be astonished—indeed, horrified! Because they did not understand this new language, they did not know what the people meant until the pagan priest arrived ready to make a sacrifice. But at this sight they ran among the people and tried to explain that they were only men. Indeed, when Paul got their attention, he turned the incident into an occasion for declaring the ways of the living God.

How fickle were those Lystrans! One day they were ready to worship the strange creature; the next, they were willing to stone him to death. Perhaps they were disgusted with themselves when they realized they had mistaken men for gods. If so, they were in a receptive mood for the persecuting Jews who had trailed Paul and Barnabas from Antioch and Iconium. As he was being battered to the ground by the stones, Paul must have thought of another stoning he had witnessed. Before he lost consciousness, Paul must have wondered whether he would suffer Stephen's fate. But the Lord had other work for Paul to do, and he gave him strength to return to the city and go on to Derbe on the next day.

6. Back to Antioch (14:21-28)

Luke did not attempt in Acts to give a day-by-day account of Paul's ministry. Instead of recounting the little triumphs or setbacks that came day by day, he told of the more dramatic incidents. But every Christian knows that his own witness must persevere through many routine days and duties when constructive but unexciting things are done for the kingdom. What a journal of personal encounters, adventures in prayer, and experiences in soul-winning must have been condensed in the words: "they had preached the gospel to that city and had made many disciples"! After all, what greater tribute could be paid to any evangelist, whether layman or preacher!

Instead of returning to their home church in Syrian Antioch by the shortest route and taking time to visit in Tarsus, the missionaries began to retrace their steps through Lystra, Iconium, and Antioch. Paul and Barnabas were more than visiting evangelists. Because of their experience in Syrian Antioch, they had the pastor's heart and viewpoint. Despite the dangers they might meet in those cities, they wanted to encourage the disciples in their new faith and strengthen them in their new way of life. For each church they appointed some elders (or pastors). "It is fairly certain that these elders were chosen to correspond in a general way with the elders in the Jewish synagogue after which the local church was largely copied as to organization and worship" (Robertson, 217).

Having secured this leadership for at least three churches, Paul and Barnabas went on to Perga and stopped for a short time to preach before sailing from the port of Attalia to Antioch. After their absence for nearly two years, Paul and Barnabas must have been greeted with great joy and heard with keen interest as they told their home church of their missionary adventures.

III. By Holding Fast the Simple Gospel (15:1-31)

Throughout this chapter we have seen that "ready" means more than being prompt and willing. The church at Antioch was ready—both prompt and willing—to send out missionaries to the Gentiles. The missionaries themselves were ready to suffer for Christ that both Jews and Gentiles might hear the gospel. But they were more than prompt and willing; they were prepared. Their experience of grace, their growing knowledge of God's will as revealed through the Scriptures and in Christ, their deepening fellowship in service with other Christians— all these prepared them to share and defend the gospel.

1. A Dispute with the Judaizers (1-5)

After Paul and Barnabas had told the Antioch Christians how the Lord "had opened the door of faith unto the Gentiles," they settled there for a good visit before making another tour. During those months came some self-appointed inspectors of orthodoxy from Jerusalem. They were not happy about the way the church had so carelessly received Gentiles into its fellowship. After all, Jesus was a Jew, and he fulfilled ancient Hebrew prophecies in his life and work. Although he opposed some interpretations of the law, he never repudiated it. He himself was obedient to it and claimed to have come to fulfil it. The law commanded circumcision for the faithful—a symbol of their devotion to Jehovah and acceptance of the Jewish way of life. Thus, to enter into fellowship of Christians, the Gentiles must first become Jews.

That was the argument of the Judaizers from Jerusalem. Paul was a "Hebrew of the Hebrews" (see Phil. 3:4-6), but he had been reborn as a Christian and called by the Spirit to preach to the Gentiles. He and Barnabas had seen God's grace work wonders in the redemption and enducment of Gentile converts. Therefore, they withstood vigorously the argument of the men from Jerusalem. They knew that salvation could not come through any ritual but only through "the door of faith." As the debate wore on and the Antioch Christians realized how it could affect their missionary program, they decided to take up the question directly with the church leaders in Jerusalem. Notice that the Jerusalem church did not send for the Antioch Christians to defend themselves. The latter went to Jerusalem of their own free will.

Of course Paul and Barnabas would not let the trip be one of business only. They probably took their time through Phenicia and Samaria and told again and again the story of their first missionary tour and how the Gentiles responded to the gospel. When they arrived in Jerusalem, they were welcomed by the church. Reports from Antioch and rumors of the first missionary tour had thrilled the hearts of the truly evangelical Christians in Jerusalem. Many still remembered vividly the way

Saul had persecuted them; now they rejoiced in what the Lord had done through him. And it was good to hear it from his own lips.

The meeting might have been a sort of missions rally except for the objection raised by some Jewish Christians who still were loyal to the pharisaic interpretation of the law. It was the same crowd that had struck the sour note in Antioch. Paul referred to them as "false brethren secretly brought in, who slipped in to spy out our freedom which we have in Christ Jesus, that they might bring us into bondage" (Gal. 2:4 RSV).

2. Discussing the Problem Openly (6-21)

Most New Testament scholars agree that Acts 15 and Galatians 2 should be read together as representing the same Jerusalem meeting. Perhaps they can best be fitted together by letting Galatians 2:1-10 be an enlargement on Acts 15:6. When the Judaizers interrupted the missions rally, Paul may have asked for a special meeting with the apostles and elders. To them he declared his convictions and his experiences (Gal. 2:2). He had not come for advice or to get a majority report from the Jerusalem church. He knew that he was on the side of the Spirit, and he would not be disobedient to his vision and commission just to keep the peace. But he did want them to understand what he had been doing and why. Before that session was over, the church leaders (James, Peter, and John) agreed on the significance of the mission to the Gentiles (Gal. 2:9).

Later the church was called together to discuss the matter in business session. Because we are so much more interested in the actual words of some of the speakers, we might be tempted to pass over lightly those words: "and after there had been much debate" (RSV). But that is a very important comment on the way this whole matter was handled. Nobody told any group how it should act; the church heard those on both sides and then made up its mind what it should do. That is true democratic procedure. Of course we do have special reference given to the words of Peter, Paul and Barnabas, and James; and they disagreed with the Judaizers. But from Luke's point of view (more than ten years later) these were the only significant comments made.

Peter was the first speaker to show the crystallizing sentiment of both the church and its leaders. He recalled the time when he was appointed to be an evangelist unto the Gentiles and how surely the Spirit had demonstrated his approval of the hearty response of the Gentiles to the free gospel. God had shown his will in the instance of Cornelius; why should they try to test him again? No one had ever been able to bear the yoke of the law which the Judaizers wanted to put on the Gentiles. Then Peter added a startling sentence: "We believe that we are saved through the grace of the Lord Jesus in like manner as they also" (Robertson, 228). Imagine saying that the Jew would be saved in the same way that the Gentile would be saved!

The Judaizers probably cried out in protest against that statement, and the other Christians may have shouted their approval. At least, Luke hints that the multitude had to become quiet before Barnabas and Paul began to tell again their experiences in winning the Gentiles to Christ.

Then to continue the presentation of the views of the Jerusalem leaders, James declared his own conviction. The Judaizers may have hoped that he would side with them, for he was looked upon as the leader of the Jerusalem church. But he began at once to offer scriptural support for Peter's witness to the Gentiles. Quoting from the Septuagint (the first Greek translation of the Old

Testament) instead of the original Hebrew, James seems to have drawn, in verses 16-18, from three different Old Testament passages (Amos 9:11-12; Jer. 12:15; Isa. 45:21). If God had thus planned for the salvation of the Gentiles, James concluded that the Jewish Christian should do nothing to trouble them but only urge them to avoid certain behavior which might be offensive to their fellow Christians and a real handicap in commending the Way unto believing Jews.

3. They Reach a Great Decision (22-31)

James seems to have summed up the judgment of the body. While some kind of vote was being taken, the Judaizers must have refused to speak or may even have walked out of the meeting; at least the sentiment favoring the free gospel seems to have been unanimous. Two leaders from their own number were selected to return with Paul and Barnabas to Antioch to take a letter of encouragement and instruction for the brethren in Antioch, Syria, and Cilicia.

First of all, they pointed out that the brethren from Jerusalem who had upset their minds did not represent the views of the Jerusalem church. To speak more at length along that line they were sending two of their leading members to visit with the Antioch church. As a further indication of their warm approval of Barnabas and Paul, they mentioned them as "our beloved" and praised them for risking their lives in the Master's service.

Then as apostles, elders, and members of the Jerusalem church they assured their Antioch brethren that the Holy Spirit had led them to hold fast the simple gospel, to commend unto them the free gospel. The only requirements they made were matters of basic morality and one item—restraining from things strangled—as a concession to Jewish feeling. No church could have asked for a finer spirit or a more courteous letter. These Christians were still being tested in their fellowship, still being obedient to divine direction, because they had been empowered by the Spirit.

Of course the Antioch Christians rejoiced in the letter and in the fellowship of their visitors from Jerusalem. They must have known that their missionary work would be greatly strengthened by the decision of the Jerusalem conference. But did they know that a great battle had been won that would save Christianity from becoming a mere sect of Judaism? Could they see that by their action in confirming the original emphasis of the gospel they would encourage Christians through the centuries to stand for salvation by grace through faith?

For Review and Further Study

1. In what three ways did first-century Christians set an example for us in sharing and defending the gospel?

2. What church took over the missionary leadership from the church in Jerusalem? Who were its appointees?

3. Why did these missionaries go first to the synagogues?

4. What emphases in Paul's first recorded sermon remind you of Stephen's defense and Peter's sermon at Pentecost? What was its distinctive theme?

5. In what ways was the ministry of Paul and Barnabas superior to that of mere traveling evangelists?

6. Who were the Judaizers?

7. What was the purpose of the conference described in Acts 15? Who were the main speakers? Why was Paul pleased with its decision?

VI

COMMITTED TO WORLD MISSIONS

Acts 15:32 to 18:22

I. *Enlisting New Workers* (15:32 to 16:10)

    1. At Work in Antioch (15:32-35)
    2. Barnabas and Paul Disagree (15:36-40)
    3. Timothy Joins the Mission (15:41 to 16:5)
    4. "A Man of Macedonia" (16:6-10)

II. *Entering New Fields* (16:11 to 17:15)

    1. Lydia, Europe's First Convert (16:11-15)
    2. Paul Interferes with Business (16:16-24)
    3. A Jailer Becomes a Christian (16:25-40)
    4. Old Opposition on a New Continent (17:1-15)

III. *Encountering Pagan Culture and Sin* (17:16 to 18:22)

    1. A Sermon for Philosophers (17:16-34)
    2. Paul Teaches in Corinth (18:1-17)
    3. The End of the Second Tour (18:18-22)

COMMITTED TO WORLD MISSIONS
Acts 15:32 to 18:22

"And unto the uttermost part of the earth"—in the echo of those words the Master left his followers on his ascension day. Yet for nearly a score of years they worked only at building up the home church and finally relinquished missionary leadership to a predominantly Gentile church.

Despite all their advantages those first-century Christians are more easily excused for their hesitation in entering upon the worldwide phase of their mission than are we. We haven't heard the commission from Jesus' lips, but it speaks with authority to us through the pages of God's Word. We have never seen him heal the sick or by his own word bring forgiveness to a sinner, but we have the testimony of nearly 2,000 years that Christ Jesus can still save sinners and build up the saved in strength. But can we say that twentieth-century Baptists are really committed to world missions when in 1949 we had only 700 missionaries and were giving only three and a half million dollars to support our whole foreign missionary program?

I. ENLISTING NEW WORKERS (15:32 to 16:10)

Of course this chapter tells the story of Paul's second missionary journey, but it starts out with two incidents from the life of the Antioch church: the ministry of Silas and the disagreement of Paul and Barnabas over Mark. Then we have the introduction of Timothy who joined the group as they left Lystra. Finally in 16:10 we discover a change in the point of view of the author of Acts. Instead of "they" he says "we." Thus, Luke must have joined Paul as he left Troas.

In a very real way, therefore, this was a time of enlisting new workers for the world missionary enterprise—a primary condition for any progress in modern missionary work. However grand may be our plans, however generous may be our gifts, however broad may be our knowledge, we cannot evangelize the world without missionaries. Great plans for missionary advancement must include missionary enlistment. Tithes and offerings must be matched with the gifts of our sons and daughters. Along with mission study must go the acceptance of the opportunity to rear missionaries in one's own family.

1. At Work in Antioch (15:32-35)

Surely Antioch's welcome for Judas and Silas was made much warmer because of the letter from Jerusalem. The Antioch brethren may have shared Paul's attitude; they wanted to have a judgment from Jerusalem on the Judaizing issue, but they did not expect to abide by that judgment if it was contrary to their own convictions. Whatever their suspicions of the Jerusalem church, the letter allayed them all. Judas and Silas gave a good account of themselves, too, as they preached and strengthened their Antioch brethren.

After they had gone, Paul and Barnabas continued with their own work of teaching and preaching. (Verse 34 does not appear in the best manuscripts.) They were missionaries and very much aware of their commission, but when they were at home, they did not stop their evangelizing. They knew what every true missionary knows: that extending the frontiers depends upon a strong home base. Notice that they combined their preaching with teaching; in fact, teaching is mentioned first.

2. Barnabas and Paul Disagree (15:36-40)

That period in Antioch, however, may also have been the time when Peter visited the Christians there. Paul told the story in Galatians 2:11-21. At first Peter was generous in his relations with the Gentile Christians, but he changed when the Judaizers threatened him. Of course Paul had to rebuke such conduct, but he found himself standing almost alone. Even Barnabas sided with Peter.

If this incident has been correctly dated, we can better understand the tension that arose between Paul and Barnabas over the latter's desire to have Mark accompany them on their next journey. But Paul remembered how Mark had turned back toward Jerusalem when they reached Pamphylia on the previous tour (13:13). He must have felt that there was something of the quitter in the younger man; for if there had been a legitimate reason for Mark's leaving the party, Paul would probably have raised no objection about his going on this second trip. Remembering the hardships and dangers of the other tour, Paul hesitated to risk another desertion on Mark's part.

But Barnabas was equally determined to have his cousin go along. The Greek word for the "sharp contention" that arose between the two leaders is the root of our word "paroxysm," convulsion or fit. We usually think that they "agreed to disagree," but the Bible does not say that. It does tell, however, through the writings of Paul how these men continued their work and held no resentment toward each other. Of course we commend Barnabas for wanting to give his cousin a second chance. On the other hand, we can hardly blame Paul for doubting a deserter. Later he came to recognize the good qualities in Mark, calling him one of his "fellow labourers" (Philem. 24) and acknowledging him as being "profitable to me for the ministry" (2 Tim. 4:11).

Through God's grace even this contention was turned to the purposes of the kingdom. For Mark was reclaimed, and Silas was enlisted as a new worker.

3. Timothy Joins the Mission (15:41 to 16:5)

Since Barnabas was returning to Cyprus, there was no need for Paul and Silas to follow the route of the first missionary journey. They turned northward from Antioch and went on foot through Syria and Cilicia. Notice Luke's passing comment that Paul strengthened the churches as he traveled. What churches? Some of them may have been established by Paul as he worked out from Antioch. Others, especially in Cilicia, must have been the fruit of his work between the time of his leaving Jerusalem (9:30) and his going to Antioch (11:25).

In Lystra our attention is focused on one young man. He and his mother had evidently been won to Christ by Paul on his previous visit. However he had been witnessing, Timothy had a good reputation in both Lystra and Iconium. Although he had been trained as a Jew, Timothy had never been acknowledged as a Jew through the ritual of circumcision, perhaps because his father was a Greek. Paul still believed that this ritual was unnecessary to the Gentile's becoming a Christian, but he saw no use in giving needless offense to Jewish Christians by having an uncircumcised Jew in his missionary party. Paul saw great promise in the young man and enlisted him as a new worker.

Then Paul, Silas, and Timothy went on to Iconium and Antioch. Not knowing the exact boundaries of the Roman privinces in Asia Minor, we cannot trace positively Paul's journey from Antioch to Troas. Perhaps they went due west from Antioch toward the borders of Asia. Then in some way the Holy Spirit forbade him to speak in Asia. When they turned northward and would have entered Bithynia, again the Spirit stood in their way. There seemed nothing else to do but turn westward toward Troas. What Christian worker is not familiar with the negative leading of the Spirit!

4. "A Man of Macedonia" (16:6-10)

In that important city, built just a few miles south of ancient Troy, Paul had a vision that helped him realize that the Spirit's two bewildering rejections of his own plans were a part of a larger plan of God. The vision that he had in Troas was almost as radical in its effect on his life as the Damascus road experience. Certainly it meant as much to the spread of Christianity as did Paul's conversion.

The Mediterranean world was fairly compact. It was unified by culture and government and trade. Geographically there wasn't much difference in the Mediterranean world between Europe and Asia. Just to the north of Troas only two miles of water separated the continents at the Dardanelles. But there was more to Europe than its Mediterranean shore line. For Paul, there were the centers of Greek culture, there was Rome itself. So far as we are concerned, his invitation to Europe was an invitation to the west—to the rest of the world.

As if the voice of that visionary Macedonian was all that he had been waiting for, Paul prepared immediately to cross the Aegean Sea to Macedonia. But he wasn't the only one who felt called to preach the gospel there. In verse 10 the writer of Acts changed from the third personal pronouns to the second person. Unto Paul, Silas, and Timothy another had been added—Luke. The great missionary had enlisted another worker!

II. Entering New Fields (16:11 to 17:15)

We don't know much about Paul's conception of the world, but it was probably no larger than that of the recognized geographers of his day. He didn't know about China, North America, or South Africa. But he did know about Italy, Macedonia, and Achaia. Palestinian Jews might think that Judea was the center of the world—about all the world worth knowing! But Jewish Christians kept hearing Jesus say, "Unto the uttermost part of the earth." They had taken quite a step in leaving Jerusalem to preach in Samaria, and another in going on to Antioch. But Paul had thrilled to the invasion of other regions. He knew that only by entering new fields could missionaries begin a conquest of the world for Christ.

Just because we know where all the continents are and have missionaries at work on all but one (Australia), we Southern Baptists have little room to boast that we are doing as well as Paul in evangelizing the world. You can study a mission map and find that out. Our 700 missionaries are scattered over the world; but if we are committed to world missions, we must begin now to enter new fields.

1. Lydia, Europe's First Convert (16:11-15)

From Troas the four missionaries sailed to Neapolis (Greek for New City), and from that port they walked on to Philippi, the most prominent city in Macedonia. Why didn't they stop at Neapolis? Perhaps for the same reason that Paul seemed to do so little work in the open country of Asia Minor. He was a city man and probably understood the city better than the open country. But more than that, he realized the significance of the larger city for the surrounding countryside. It was the center for distribution of goods and ideas. To the cities the farmers would come for festivals and market days. From the cities men would go to smaller towns and carry the message of Christ.

When Paul found no synagogue in Philippi, he and his party waited until the sabbath and went outside the city to find a likely place of prayer beside a river (a favorite place for Jewish worship when no synagogue could be built). Could those women that they found be the "man of Macedonia"? And why not? Women had no prominent place in official Judaism, but Paul knew something of their service to Christ in his earthly life, and he had seen their loyalty to the Lord under persecution. The missionaries did not hesitate to sit down (as ancient teachers always did) and begin to speak of Christ to those women.

Lydia was a Gentile proselyte and evidently a woman of some prominence; for she was a merchant and her home was large enough to entertain Paul and his fellow workers. Just as the Spirit had led the missionaries to Philippi, he also led Lydia to find in Christ the salvation she had sought. Evidently she led her household (family, servants, or both) to the same decision because they were all baptized. Even though her name is never mentioned again in the New Testament, she must have become a leading spirit in the church that would give Paul so much joy in later years.

2. Paul Interferes with Business (16:16-24)

We do not know how long the missionaries stayed in Philippi, but we do know when they left. Certainly they were in the city long enough to get a church established and to gain for themselves a reputation as teachers of unlawful customs (16:20-21). For many days Paul and his companions were followed along the streets of Philippi by a slave girl, shouting, "These men are servants of the

Most High God, who proclaim unto you the way of salvation." Realizing that she was demon-possessed and being used by some men to make money, Paul became annoyed with her cries and indignant about her condition. Suddenly one day he turned and spoke to the evil spirit in the name of Christ. Immediately the girl was delivered from her possession by evil.

Her deliverance meant that she would be of no more profit to her owners, and they did not rejoice when Paul freed her from the demon. Paul had touched them in their tenderest spot. A person is worth far more than he can earn. In God's sight a man has more value than all the wealth of the world. We don't expect those pagan Greeks to believe and practice that, but Christians—children of God!—must love one another as they love themselves. They must be just as concerned about the health, education, safety, working, and living conditions of others as they are about their own.

Instead of rejoicing in what had been done for their slave, her owners grabbed Paul and Silas and hailed them into court. But notice that they did not mention to the rulers their real grievance against the missionaries. Instead, the first appealed to prejudice ("these men, being Jews") and then accused them of preaching an illegal religion. The mob responded violently to this appeal to racial and national prejudice. The rulers acquiesced then to the mind of the mob and had Paul and Silas beaten and thrown in jail. What a childish way to deal with God's truth!

So far as we know this is the first time that the gospel according to Paul ran counter to the business of making money, but it would not be the last time! The real gospel always speaks against making money at another's expense.

3. A Jailer Becomes a Christian (16:25-40)

What did Paul and Silas receive in return for their kindness to the slave girl? Torn clothes, bleeding backs, a pitch-black prison cell, and tightly-fastened stocks on their feet. Was that the way for missionaries to be treated? A sinful world will always try to escape the gospel by trying to silence it. But even in a dungeon the good news broke forth in song! Other prisoners listened to those two men singing and praying in the blackness. Were they just "whistling in the dark"? No, there was another note in their singing. They were rejoicing in their privilege to suffer for Christ; they were praying for strength to keep on being loyal at any cost.

Suddenly in the midst of that prayer and praise service the prisoners felt the earth tremble beneath them. They felt the great stones in the walls shudder. Then doors began to fall from their hinges; stocks pulled loose; chains lost their moorings. Through an open door Paul saw the jailer ready to kill himself when he thought his prisoners had escaped. Only Paul's reassurance restrained the jailer from suicide.

Although the jailer could not see the speaker, he must have recognized the voice. And the Spirit of God led him to ask one of the greatest questions of all time—a question of sincere conviction, of humble seeking, of anxious readiness. How can some say that the jailer only feared the wrath of the magistrates? Why, he already knew his prisoners were safe. That was not the burden of his question. He saw himself condemned before the great Judge and felt that these men were messengers of a wondrous salvation. His question was all the invitation that Paul and Silas needed to declare the gospel. The Spirit used their teaching to bring the jailer and his household to saving faith—the kind "that laid hold on the Lord Jesus" (Carver, 171). Then the saved man acted like a saved man; notice all that he did.

During the night the magistrates must have realized how unjustly they had treated Paul and Silas. But admitting their mistake publicly would have brought embarrassment; therefore they sent word that the prisoners should be released quietly. Paul must have realized the situation immediately, for he decided to take advantage of it. Speaking directly to the police, Paul listed the ways in which the missionaries had been treated unjustly. Strangely enough, the magistrates did just what Paul demanded: "They came and apologized to them. And they took them out and asked them to leave the city" (RSV).

Perhaps Paul left Luke to work with the Philippian church. At least, from now until 20:5 the author used "they" instead of "we." He must have done a good work there; for "it proved Paul's most gratifying church, liberal, loyal, progressive and free from any serious heresies" (Carver, 172).

4. Old Opposition on a New Continent (17:1-15)

Even though beaten and imprisoned, the missionaries had fared better in Philippi at the hands of Gentiles than they had in Lystra at the hands of the Jews. Paul may have hoped that the Jews in Macedonia would be more receptive to the gospel. Certainly he did not forget their need. He and Silas began their work in Thessalonica in the synagogue. For three weeks (or sabbaths) Paul used a synagogue to present the gospel. Since his hearers were well acquainted with the Scriptures (the Old Testament), he used them to make clear the character of the Christ and then proved that Jesus of Nazareth, by all that he said and did, was the Messiah. A few of the Jews were convinced, but a multitude of the God-fearing Gentiles joined with Paul and Silas.

As in Pisidian Antioch, the Jews of Thessalonica were jealous "when they saw their influential Gentile sympathizers, whom they had yet been unable to bring fully to Judaism, so easily won by the gospel preachers" (Carver, 173). Since they were so few in such a large city, the Jews could hardly hope for a favorable hearing against the missionaries in a local Roman court. Thus they decided to use any help they could get with money or persuasion. Incited by some rough idlers from the market place, a boisterous mob dragged Jason and some other Christians before the rulers of the city with a remarkable charge: Jason had been sheltering those who had "turned the world upside down" and were acting disloyally to Caesar.

To cloud the issue, the Jews were blaming Paul and Silas for the very uproar which they themselves had incited. Yet they spoke a truth which they did not realize. For in the midst of the ever-sinful world the way of Christ is always revolutionary; it is always opposed to man-made things-as-they-are.

Even though the rulers of the city released Jason and the other Christians, the church sent Paul and Silas to Berea, about fifty miles away. Again they went to the synagogue to declare their message, and in that small town they found a new attitude on the part of the Jews. They were willing not only to hear Paul's explanation but also to study the Scriptures for themselves. In the light of that exercise, Luke rightly used "therefore" when telling how heartily both Jews and Greeks responded to the gospel.

III. Encountering Pagan Culture and Sin (17:16 to 18:22)

Missionary work cannot be done in a vacuum—simply because the lost don't live in a vacuum. They have their own ideas about God and man, their own attitudes toward them. Whether they live in exclusive Heather Heights or on an Indian reservation, whether they teach in a European university or farm in the African bush, they have some kind of religious inclination, some kind of world outlook.

The missionary on the foreign field and the soul-winner in the local home church must become acquainted with the religion and world outlook of those whom they would win to Christ. Until the soul-winner becomes somewhat familiar with the thought world of the lost person, he'll not have much success in bringing him to a saving faith in Christ. Christians who are committed to world missions, therefore, must be willing and able to encounter—as in a conflict—pagan culture and sin.

1. A Sermon for Philosophers (17:16-34)

Some men and women might be fully equipped along these lines to serve as missionaries and yet lack one essential element. They might not be willing to *encounter* pagan culture and sin, to pit Christian faith and practice against the quaint or vicious customs of the lost. Having that element made a missionary out of Paul. Successful or unsuccessful, he was willing to show the Jews the inadequacy of their faith and to show the pagans the error of their ways.

It was while waiting in Athens that Paul met perhaps his severest test in dealing with pagan culture. For 500 years that city had been the center of art and philosophy in the Mediterranean world. But in Paul's day the city had little left except pride in its

Fool

past. Its religion was bankrupt; its philosophers spent their time in shallow argumentation.

Ever since Paul had noticed a great number of idols in Athens, he had been preaching the gospel in the synagogue to Jews and God-fearers. Then between sabbaths he talked publicly with any who would listen in the manner of the Greek teachers. Some of the philosophers themselves stopped in to hear what Paul had to say. Some called him a "picker up of seeds" (babbler); others seemed to think that he was preaching about two new gods: Jesus and the resurrection.

Although Paul was not arrested, he was taken before the Areopagus, a sort of court for examining new teachers and teachings. ("Areopagus" means hill of Ares, the Greek name for Mars.) The court invited him to explain his teaching, and Paul responded in brilliant fashion. First, he commended them for being very religious (rather than "too superstitious" as in the KJV). Among the many statues and idols, he had noticed one altar inscribed "To an Unknown God." Evidently the Athenians feared they might have overlooked one of the gods and set up that altar to prevent his vengeance. And they *had* overlooked one—"God that made the world and all things therein." With such a masterful introduction Paul immediately had the attention of the court. But more than that, by identifying his message with the Greeks' concern for "an unknown God," Paul saved himself from the charge of teaching a new religion.

Paul's address before the Areopagus revealed his consummate skill as a missionary. Not only did he understand the relationship of the gospel to basic conceptions of pagan philosophy, but he was also able to make clear that relationship. As creator and sustainer of all things, God could not possibly be housed in man-made temples, nor could he be served physically as if he needed anything. As he had created heaven and earth, so had "he made of one every nation of men to dwell on all the face of the earth" (ASV). This wasn't a new doctrine for the Greeks, for several of their own poets had expressed the sentiments in verse 28. If we are the offspring of God, he cannot be like the idols of the Greeks. Such ignorance God had overlooked in the past, but now he had fixed a day of judgment and appointed a man to judge the world—a Man approved of God by being raised from the dead.

Of course Paul intended to go on from there to present the basic facts of the gospel in the person and works of Jesus. But he didn't get a chance, for the Athenians stumbled mentally over the idea of the resurrection of the dead. Some of them ridiculed; others were more polite in dismissing him. It was an embarrassing defeat for the vigorous and brilliant preacher, but at least one of the court joined him along with a few others in the city.

2. Paul Teaches in Corinth (18:1-17)

From the cultural center of Greece Paul went next to its commercial capital. There he faced another kind of opposition: the atmosphere of vice and materialism. Again he turned first to the Jews, found lodging with a couple recently expelled from Rome, and worked with them at his trade of tentmaking. On the sabbath he continued in the synagogue to explain the Scriptures in the light of Jesus and to present Christ's claims in the light of the Scriptures. Perhaps at first he was only preparing the way; but when Silas and Timothy arrived from Macedonia, he identified Jesus as the Christ. Even after his teaching the majority of the Jews were not ready for that declaration; "they opposed and reviled him" so vehemently that Paul dramatically rejected them and turned to the Gentiles.

That was no mistake. One Gentile God-fearer gave him shelter and a place to speak. Then the ruler of the synagogue made a profession of faith along with his family. In the midst of the subsequent revival the Lord appeared to Paul to bolster his courage for a fruitful two-year ministry in Corinth.

Notice what he was doing all that time: "teaching the word of God." We expect the workers with children and young people to teach. Parents also must teach. But the evangelist, too, must teach as well as preach. The missionary and personal soul-winner must be teachers. Certainly the evangelistic zeal of Paul, Silas, and Timothy cannot be questioned. In that, they set twentieth-century Christians a glowing example. From a human point of view, however, the success and permanence of their work resulted from combining teaching with preaching.

Because of Gallio's kindly disposition, the Jews may have thought that during his proconsulship (A.D. 51-52) they might rid the city of the Christian missionaries. But when he discovered that their charges against Paul had to do only with one Jew's teaching other Jews a new way to worship their own God, he dismissed the case. He refused to get entangled in a Jewish dispute that involved no item of Roman law. Perhaps because they had been duped by their leaders, the Jewish mob (not "the Greeks" as in KJV) gave their synagogue ruler a beating.

Luke's comment about Gallio in verse 17 is "often misunderstood as a description of Gallio's lack of interest in Christianity, a religious indifferentist. . . . Gallio shows up well in Luke's narrative as a clear-headed judge who would not be led astray by Jewish

subterfuges and with the courage to dismiss a mob"
(Robertson, 302-303).

3. The End of the Second Tour (18:18-22)

For once in his ministry Paul had not been forced to
leave a community just because the Jews rose up against
him. He stayed "yet a good while" in Corinth. Then accompanied by his good friends, Aquila and Priscilla, he
sailed for Syria. When they reached Ephesus, Paul stayed
long enough to visit the synagogue and sort of introduce
his message by reasoning with the Jews there. Despite
their friendly interest Paul declined their invitation to
stay with them longer. But he promised to return. Ephesus would be the heart of his third missionary journey.

From Ephesus he sailed to Caesarea, the principal port
of Palestine, and went from there to Jerusalem to greet
the church. After perhaps a short visit there recounting
to the sympathetic brethren the progress of the gospel on
two continents, he made the long journey northward to
Antioch, his home base.

Thus Paul's second missionary journey came to an end.
A new continent had been entered for organized evangelistic effort. On the mount of ascension the Christians
had been commissioned, but now they were committed:
to world missions.

For Review and Further Study

1. Name the four workers enlisted by Barnabas and Paul.
2. Trace on a map Paul's second missionary journey.
3. How was the vision at Troas a turning point in Paul's ministry
   and in the progress of the gospel?
4. What were the three main events of Paul's ministry in Philippi?
5. Why is the story of the Philippian jailer's conversion used so
   frequently by those who seek to win the lost?
6. What remarkable charge did the Thessalonian Jews bring
   against Paul and Silas? In what way was it true?
7. What essential element do some Christians lack for being soul-
   winners?

VII

DILIGENT IN WINNING
AND TRAINING OTHERS

Acts 18:23 to 21:16

I. *For the Spirit's Use* (18:23 to 19:7)

    1. Two Disciples Instruct a Missionary (18:23-28)
    2. Others Receive the Holy Spirit (19:1-7)

II. *For Loyalty to Truth* (19:8-41)

    1. Paul Begins His Work in Ephesus (8-12)
    2. Burning the Books of Magic (13-20)
    3. In Conflict with Idol Makers (21-41)

III. *For a Constant Witness* (20:1 to 21:16)

    1. Paul Visits Macedonia and Greece (20:1-5)
    2. From Philippi to Miletus (20:6-16)
    3. Farewell to the Ephesian Elders (20:17-38)
    4. On to Jerusalem (21:1-16)

VII

DILIGENT IN WINNING
AND TRAINING OTHERS

Acts 18:23 to 21:16

Several times already in this study we have noticed
that Luke described the missionaries' work as "teaching."
That fact has been given special attention because so
many earnest Christians forget that leading men to saving faith in Christ requires more than a vigorous evangelistic sermon. Those early Christians were empowered by
the Spirit that they might be zealous in witnessing. They
were effective soul-winners at home, but they were also
committed to world missions. Both by grace and by good
common sense they saw that their work would never
amount to anything unless they followed their soul-
winning with sound teaching.

Modern Christians, too, must learn to interpret the
Bible according to Christ. That is the basic purpose of
the Sunday school. Understanding the Bible according
to Christ should help a person live according to Christ
in the fellowship of the church. But that fellowship is
so different from every other human organization that
the Christian must be trained in church membership—
the goal of the Training Union. Pity the Christian and
the church that never gives beyond its own needs, that
never sees beyond its own community, that has no group
to call attention to the frontiers of gospel witness and
service—the fundamental task of Woman's Missionary
Union.

Through these and other channels modern Christians
and churches must continue diligent in winning and training others.

Have you yielded to Him and allow Him to do the Work in us.

I. FOR THE SPIRIT'S USE (18:23 to 19:7)

How do you know Have Power.

If our lives are successful Words come freely and I concerned

This chapter tells the story of Paul's third missionary journey, and on this one he started out alone. It ends with his last fateful journey to Jerusalem. In all things Paul put himself at the disposal of the Spirit. For him the Spirit was a living Presence, empowering, guiding, and encouraging the Christian. For him the Christian could not do the work of witnessing until the Spirit had come upon him. Only the Spirit can make clear the Scriptures. Only the Spirit can motivate a man to live by love—and show him how to do it. Only the Spirit can prepare the Christian to be a winning witness.

Thus, Paul and his followers were concerned that every believer be trained for the Spirit's use. Southern Baptists by the hundreds of thousands need that kind of training today.

1. Two Disciples Instruct a Missionary (18:23-28)

How much is condensed into verse 23 no one can say. After spending some time in Antioch reporting to the brethren the progress of the new work in Europe and perhaps working with them as he had on his previous furlough, Paul struck northward again through Cilicia into Galatia. "Strengthening all the disciples" was probably done with expository preaching, personal conferences, Bible teaching, and the enlistment of leaders.

Then Luke interrupted the story of Paul to introduce a new missionary. Apollos was a Jew born in Alexandria, Egypt. We don't know where Apollos had heard of Jesus, but he had not heard enough. He knew and believed enough to teach "accurately the things concerning Jesus" (RSV), but he knew only the baptism of John. That may mean (1) that he knew only the baptism of repentance and nothing about the cross and resurrection or (2) that he knew nothing about the baptism of the Holy Spirit.

The latter seems more probable; else why should he be described as "instructed in the way of the Lord" and teaching "accurately the things concerning Jesus"?

Priscilla and Aquila realized what he lacked and perhaps what he might become; instead of denouncing his half gospel, they took him aside and taught him more fully. Be it ever remembered to Apollos' credit that the bold and eloquent witness, the mighty student of the Scriptures was willing to be taught! So eagerly and well did he learn that when he decided to go to Corinth, his Ephesian brethren wrote a good letter of commendation for him. And there he had a most useful ministry.

2. Others Receive the Holy Spirit (19:1-7)

Luke's interruption to introduce Apollos was necessary because of his subsequent ministry in Corinth and Paul's relation to it. But in recounting the story of Apollos and his limitation in understanding the gospel, Luke may have been reminded of a similar case in Paul's experience at Ephesus. Sometime after reaching the key city for his third tour, Paul talked with about a dozen men who frankly declared: "We have never even heard that there is a Holy Spirit" (RSV). Most scholars agree that they were disciples of John the Baptist. At least they claimed to have been baptized "unto John's baptism."

Then Paul explained the significance of John's baptism something like this: "John indeed preached repentance and a Saviour to come (as you know); but the Messiah whom he announced has appeared in Jesus, and you are now to believe on him as John directed" (Hackett, 219). One was the baptism of repentance and anticipated salvation; the other is the baptism of accomplished salvation. Some might point to this incident as an argument for rebaptism. There may be many immersions, but there is only one baptism. Baptism is immersion with a unique significance. It is a symbolic testimony to a spiritual experience.

II. FOR LOYALTY TO TRUTH (19:8-41)

Even non-Christians like to quote Jesus' famous saying: "Ye shall know the truth, and the truth shall make you free" (John 8:32). But they usually ignore the preceding verse, which suggests the source of "the truth" and the people who can know it. God's truth has its origin in Jesus Christ. Until a man knows him, he cannot know truth at its core.

On the other hand, many Christian people treat carelessly the latter half of John 8:32. They haven't the faith to be loyal to the truth, and only to the truth. They substitute some tradition like infant baptism for the truth that Christ proclaimed. They look to the childish schemes of men—astrology, palmistry, numerology—instead of the truth of God's providence and care. They let a greedy human nature determine their concern for other people instead of living by a growing love—the heart of God's truth.

1. Paul Begins His Work in Ephesus (8-12)

Paul had looked forward to returning to Ephesus ever since he had been received there so kindly when on his way to Jerusalem at the end of his second journey. He was pleased with the response of the Jews, but more than that, he recognized the potential significance of Ephesus as a Christian center. It was the political, commercial, and cultural capital of the entire province of Asia. Paul worked there longer than in any other city; his Ephesian ministry may well be accounted the climax of his missionary work.

Because of the Jews' previous interest and courtesy and because of Paul's concern for his own people, he went first to the synagogue. For three months he was free to discuss the person and work of Jesus in the light of the Old Testament and the Jewish anticipation of the kingdom of God. But finally some of the Jews began to realize what this gospel would mean to their legalistic interpretation of the relationship with God. When they began to speak evil of the Way, Paul moved his discussions in the lecture hall of Tyrannus. Paul met his followers there in the hours when Tyrannus was not teaching, perhaps 11:00 A.M. to 4:00 P.M. That arrangement continued for two years.

In addition to his teaching Paul worked at his trade to support himself and led religious services in the homes of believers. His Ephesian days were full, but they were also fruitful! From Ephesus the gospel was proclaimed throughout the province of Asia.

Along with his teaching and preaching Paul performed some special miracles by the power of God. We remember the case of Peter and his shadow (5:15) when we read of those who used handkerchiefs and aprons to help their faith. But notice that Luke only mentions these miracles; he saw them as normal evidence of the Spirit's work but as less important than Paul's conflict with superstition and idolatry.

2. Burning the Books of Magic (13-20)

Not all of those who watched Paul heal the sick were concerned for their loved ones' sake. Some had heard of his marvelous power and hoped to appropriate it for themselves. Some strolling Jews made their living as exorcists; that is, they claimed to rid people of evil spirits by using a formal oath as a spell or charm. Thus, they thought that there was some power in merely calling Jesus' name.

But the first time they tried what they thought was a magic formula, they got a big surprise. The evil spirit in the possessed man cried out, "Jesus I know [recognize], and Paul I know [am acquainted with]; but who are ye?" Then in a fury the man jumped upon the two pretenders and gave them a fearful beating.

As news of the exorcists' failure spread through the city, both unbelieving Jews and Greeks were awed by the name of Jesus Christ. But this was a time for believers, too, to take stock of themselves and make some confessions. In the midst of their pagan environment those new Christians had found it difficult to rid themselves of pagan superstitions and practices. Paul is not mentioned as guiding or exhorting them, but surely he must have helped them discover the error of their ways. To prove their renunciation of the "magical arts" (ASV), those who practiced them (whether Christians we do not know) threw their books on a ten-thousand-dollar bonfire.

In an age of so much ignorance about the physical world and human personality perhaps some superstition might be excused. But it wasn't! Christians were expected to put their faith in God and discover truth through Christ. Nor can the modern Christian be excused for remaining childish in his faith and letting superstition rule part of his life.

3. In Conflict with Idol Makers (21-41)

After nearly three years of work in Ephesus, Paul was led by the Spirit to look forward to extending his ministry as far as Rome. Of course his present tour could not be complete without his visiting Macedonia and Achaia. From the churches visited on this tour he expected to take an offering to the brethren at Jerusalem to demonstrate further the true fruit of the gospel among the Gentiles. Timothy and Erastus were sent ahead to prepare the churches for Paul's coming.

Evidently Paul thought that another great witnessing opportunity was opening up for him in Ephesus (1 Cor. 16:8-9), but he must have been disappointed. The bonfire of magic books represented a great victory of truth over superstition and ignorance, but it also set the stage for a greater test of the gospel's witnesses.

Greeks and Romans worshiped many gods, but various cities had their favorite deities. For centuries Artemis (later identified with the Roman goddess Diana) had been worshiped especially by the Ephesians. Just outside their city was a majestic white marble temple dedicated to her service and housing a great statue of the goddess. In many ways it was the heart of the city's life. To show their allegiance to their goddess, the Ephesians were glad to buy small replicas of the temple or the statue.

Hearing of Paul's teaching and of his influence in the bonfire of magic books, Demetrius, a leader among the idol makers, saw the handwriting of judgment on the wall. And he told his fellow craftsmen (or perhaps employees) what he saw and what it meant. First, he reminded them that they made money—and plenty of it! —by making shrines. Second, he pointed out the threat to their trade that Paul's teaching had become. Then very shrewdly he expressed the fear that such teaching would destroy the worship of Artemis. And finally, he claimed that Artemis was worshiped by all ages and the world, hinting that Paul was attacking the religion of practically all people. No wonder those men became enraged and turned the city into confusion. Their emotions had been manhandled by a first-class agitator.

The mob swirled like angry flood waters through the streets carrying everyone on its tide and finally pouring into the great open air theater (seating perhaps 50,000). Although they did not kill Paul's companions or do more than howl down Alexander (whose purpose we do not understand), one speech by the wrong man might have turned them to murder. Most of them didn't know why they were there, but for two hours they shouted their monotonous praise of Artemis. Not until the mayor appeared on the rostrum did the throng begin to quiet down. He asked why they made such an outcry when everyone already knew that Artemis was the goddess of Ephesus. He denied that the Christians had made any attack on their religion but said that the courts would be glad to hear the complaint of Demetrius or of any other man. Hinting that Rome might misunderstand the significance of their assembly, he dismissed the people.

Although Paul had no part in this little drama, it was his faithful witness to Christ that led to the outbreak. Whenever the full gospel is preached, it hurls a challenge to every idol maker and idol worshiper. The idol may sit on a kitchen shelf in China or Africa. It may draw interest compounded semiannually in some neighborhood bank of America. It may demand the latest fashions, the most glamorous cosmetics, slavish admiration, and a variety of luxuries. The idol may be an ugly image, a growing bank account, or a case of personal vanity. But ultimately the gospel will require of the Christian a test of his loyalty to *the* truth.

III. For a Constant Witness (20:1 to 21:16)

Paul knew that the gospel would always be in conflict with idol makers. He did not know just how or when it would break out in any particular place, but a large part of his purpose in this third missionary journey was to exhort the brethren to give an unwavering faithful witness to the gospel. Against idolaters, Judaizers, and evil tempters he urged the Christians of Asia and Europe to stand firm. In one sense it was his last message to many churches, but it had been his message from the first. Even as he taught new converts, he was training them to be constant witnesses.

Through exhortation a man may seem to have all his devotion bound into one unwavering passion for the gospel. But quiet hours of worship, regular occasions for Bible study, and even routine responsibilities in church membership—these, too, prepare the Christian for the daily tests of his loyalty to Christ.

1. Paul Visits Macedonia and Greece (20:1-5)

Again we have much work condensed into a few verses. From references in several of Paul's letters we gain some sidelights on that trip. Sometimes near the close of his stay in Ephesus he had written 1 Corinthians and sent it to the church by Timothy, hoping to solve a factional dispute there and answer various questions raised by the Corinthians. When neither the letter nor the messenger was successful, Paul seems to have written while in Macedonia another letter to Corinth, this time sent by Titus. It was during what may have been a year's stay in Macedonia that he preached as far west as Illyricum (on the Adriatic Sea) and wrote a third letter to the church at Corinth, our 2 Corinthians.

When the Corinthian letters seemed to have done their work, Paul left Macedonia for Corinth. He was there during three winter months, evidently enjoying his ministry in a peaceful church. Part of his time there was given to writing the epistle to the Romans. Although he hoped eventually to preach in the Empire's capital, his recognition of the Judaizers' stubborn hatred made him wonder whether he would ever get to Rome. The epistle might have to represent him.

To allay any suspicion as to his use of the collection he had made among the mission churches for the brethren in Jerusalem, Paul asked each church to appoint a representative to accompany the gift to Jerusalem. His missionary group had become rather large, therefore, by the time they reached Troas on the way home.

2. From Philippi to Miletus (20:6-16)

Escaping from the Jewish plot in Corinth, Paul returned through Macedonia to Philippi. There he met his good friend Luke (notice change of pronoun in verse 5) and celebrated the Passover before sailing to Troas. Here we have our first mention of a church in Troas; this is also our first reference to Christian worship services being held on the first day of the week, the Lord's Day, instead of the sabbath.

The Christians had met with their visitors in an upper room for the Lord's Supper, and Paul took that opportunity to preach to them. We don't know when he began, but he was still preaching at midnight. Suddenly the service was interrupted when a young listener tumbled out a third-story window. The light and heat of the lamps plus the lateness of the hour was more than he could bear. The congregation was shocked to find him dead, but their preacher acted in the power of the Spirit and restored the young man to life. With much rejoicing the congregation reassembled, observed the Lord's Supper, ate a meal together, and then listened as Paul continued to talk until daybreak.

Either wanting some time alone or feeling the need of vigorous exercise, Paul walked the twenty miles from Troas to Assos while the ship sailed forty miles around the cape to that port. Then in easy stages (and perhaps in a chartered boat) the group sailed to Miletus.

3. Farewell to the Ephesian Elders (20:17-38)

Pentecost was only a month away, and Paul wanted to celebrate that feast in Jerusalem. Therefore, he had not planned to stop in Ephesus for fear of taking up too much time in Asia. To take the place of that visit, he asked the Ephesian elders to visit him in Miletus.

When the elders had gathered, Paul delivered an address, which might have been entitled "On Being Faithful as a Christian Leader." Scholars are agreed that this rather short speech is unique in its revelation of the inner Paul. In it we see the pastor-missionary pouring out his heart to fellow pastors and church workers. However Luke made his notes for this speech, perhaps in shorthand, it is Paul and not Luke who is speaking.

First, Paul described his own ministry among them in Ephesus. He had not had an easy time because of Jewish plots, but in humility and earnestness he had declared the full gospel to them in public meetings and in home services. To both Jews and Greeks he had preached a gospel of "repentance toward God, and faith toward our Lord Jesus Christ." In spite of this faithfulness, he knew that in Jerusalem there was much opposition to him. Yet he felt compelled to go to Jerusalem, despite the Spirit's testimony that "bonds and afflictions" awaited him there. But not even threats against his life could deter him; for his only desire was to continue "to testify to the gospel of the grace of God" (RSV). Since he felt that he would not be meeting those elders again, he wanted them to know that he had never held back the gospel from either Jew or Gentile.

Then Paul turned to the needs of the elders. By the Holy Spirit had they been made overseers of the church.

The word for "overseers" *(episkopous)* is also translated "bishops." Used interchangeably with "elders," "bishops" is equivalent to our "pastors." They were to "shepherd" (better than "feed") the church purchased with God's own blood or "by means of the blood of him who was his own" (Carver, 205). Paul felt that the time was not far off when the faithfulness of the elders as shepherds would be tested severely.

After commending them to God who could build them up and give them their inheritance among those who were set apart in Christ, Paul indirectly warned them against greed and laziness by recalling his own example among them. Then the whole group kneeled while Paul "prayed with them all." It was a touching farewell showing something of the strong and beautiful relationship that may be developed between pastor-missionary and his fellow workers.

4. On to Jerusalem (21:1-16)

In one sense, Paul had been returning to Jerusalem ever since he left Corinth. But really from there to Miletus he continued with his missionary work. At Miletus he began his return trip, and the journey can be followed easily on a Bible map of the Mediterranean. Their ship put in at Tyre, and the missionary party visited with Christians there for a week. Again Paul had an indication that all would not be well for him in Jerusalem. This warning may have seemed more ominous since it came when Paul was closer home.

Two days later they were in Caesarea where they were guests of "Philip the evangelist, which was one of the seven." After winning the Ethiopian eunuch to Christ, Philip had preached in various coastal towns "till he came to Caesarea" (8:40). There he had centered his ministry for more than twenty years. Furthermore Philip had four young daughters, whom he had brought up in the admonition of the Lord and whom the Spirit had endowed with the gift of prophecy.

While the missionary party stayed some days (not "many days") in Philip's home, the Judean prophet Agabus come to Caesarea. (See 11:28.) In the manner of the Old Testament prophets he dramatized his message to Paul—a message of arrest and betrayal. Certainly his was a forbidding picture of Paul's fate in Jerusalem, and both the missionary party and the Christians of Caesarea urged Paul not to go to Jerusalem. Then in a sublime dedication of himself to this new venture, the great missionary made it clear that he was trying to obey the will of God.

Accompanied by some of the brethren from Caesarea, the missionary party went on up to Jerusalem with a generous offering for the brethren and with a leader who was willing to risk his life that he might be a constant witness to the gospel of Jesus Christ.

FOR REVIEW AND FURTHER STUDY

1. In knowing only the baptism of John, what did Apollos lack? For whom did he set an example in his willingness to be taught by Priscilla and Aquila?

2. What city was the focal point of Paul's third missionary journey? What two outstanding events in Paul's ministry occurred there?

3. Why do some Christians hold on to superstition and get tricked by astrology, numerology, and the like?

4. Whenever the full gospel is preached, it hurls a challenge to every idol maker and idol worshiper. Why? What idols does it challenge in your community?

5. List several things we learn about Paul, the pastor-missionary, from his farewell to the Ephesian elders.

VIII

BOLD IN DECLARING THE FAITH

Acts 21:17 to 25:12

I. *To Win the Unreconciled* (21:17 to 22:29)

1. Paul Tries to Make Peace (21:17-26)
2. Mobbed and Arrested (21:27-40)
3. Paul's Defense on the Stairs (22:1-21)
4. Saved from Scourging (22:22-29)

II. *To Preserve the Witness* (22:30 to 23:35)

1. Paul Divides the Sanhedrin (22:30 to 23:11)
2. The Jews Plan an Ambush (23:12-22)
3. To Caesarea for Safety's Sake (23:23-35)

III. *To Secure a Fair Hearing* (24:1 to 25:12)

1. Paul's Trial Before Felix (24:1-22)
2. Two Years in Prison (24:23-27)
3. Paul Appeals to Caesar (25:1-12)

VIII

BOLD IN DECLARING THE FAITH

Acts 21:17 to 25:12

Perhaps we had better take time to answer the question, Why was Paul so anxious to go to Jerusalem? Certainly it was not just to celebrate Pentecost. Nor was he primarily intent on delivering the offering from the mission churches.

On many occasions in his ministry Paul had become aware of two Jewish interpretations of Christianity. One saw it as vitally related to the Old Testament but free in its fellowship and in its faith in Christ. The other view (that of the Judaizers) saw Jesus as the consummation of the Old Testament but subordinate to its law and ritual. If the latter group prevailed, Christianity would become no more than a sect of Judaism. Even if the former group proved the stronger, the Christian movement *might* become fatally divided. Paul hoped to prevent that split through his own testimony and the generous welfare gifts from the mission churches.

Thus Paul's boldness in declaring the faith as pictured in this section is not the daring of evangelism but the courage of conviction. That kind of courage is needed in our day when men try to pervert the gospel. Evangelist, missionary, and soul-winner must know what they believe and make it plain to both Christian and non-Christian. For even in being bold to declare the faith, they may help other Christians to become better witnesses, lead nominal Christians to re-examine their profession of faith, and win the lost.

I. To Win the Unreconciled (21:17 to 22:29)

Because it is made up of human beings who sometimes see the same thing in a slightly different light, every church will sometime in its history suffer some division of opinion. That was the situation which Paul faced in Jerusalem, except that the problem was much more significant than most of the ones which divide modern churches. Refusing only to compromise his convictions, Paul was willing to do anything to win the unreconciled. He hoped that truth and generosity would gain that end. And it did eventually. But it cost Paul several years of imprisonment and finally life itself—a small price to pay for defending the true gospel.

1. Paul Tries to Make Peace (21:17-26)

Paul's missionary party was received enthusiastically by the brethren in Jerusalem. Evidently Mnason, Paul's host in Jerusalem (21:16), knew where to go so that Paul would not immediately have to encounter any Judaizers. We notice with relief, too, that there were no Judaizers among the elders of the Jerusalem church. To them Paul told the full story of his ministry among the Gentiles, and they received the news with thanksgiving to God.

Then in more solemn tones they outlined to Paul a new problem that had arisen out of his foreign mission work. It was new and yet related to the old problem settled in the Jerusalem conference ten years before. Now the Judaizers were telling the myriads of Jewish believers that Paul was instructing his Jewish converts in Asia and Europe to forsake the law of Moses. Of course the charge was untrue, but that didn't prevent the zealots of the law from believing it.

Anxious to preserve peace within the church and to give Paul a chance to make clear his position, the elders made a request of Paul. Four of the brethren had taken a vow (probably that of the Nazirite [Nazarite] described in Num. 6:1-21), and the time was near for them to conclude their period of separation with offerings at the Temple. Paul was asked to serve as their sponsor, going through part of the ritual and paying the cost of sacrifices and Temple exercises. In that voluntary service he would prove his loyalty to the Mosiac code and still not compromise his faith in Christ. When the elders reaffirmed their judgment about Gentile Christians' freedom from the law, Paul agreed to their plan.

2. Mobbed and Arrested (21:27-40)

We don't know how well the Judaizers responded to Paul's peacemaking plan, for near the end of the Temple exercises another group entered violently into the picture. Some Jews of Asia, perhaps of Ephesus, had seen him in Jerusalem with Trophimus of Ephesus and suspected that Paul had brought him at some time into the Temple. They grabbed Paul and began to accuse him as a traitor. The noisy crowd that began to gather at that alarm moved ominously through the Temple gate intent on murder. A Jew who disowned his own people, the law, and the Temple deserved death at once!

At the northwest corner of the Temple area was a castle called the Tower of Antonia. It was headquarters for the Roman garrison of Jerusalem and was connected by a stairway to the Temple area for the very purpose of preventing trouble in that center of Jewish life. At the news of the riot the Roman military tribune or colonel, Claudius Lysias, called out a guard of soldiers and officers to break up the disturbance. When the colonel tried to find out something about Paul, he could not understand the clamor of accusations. But when he ordered Paul to be taken to the castle, the mob tried so viciously

to get the prisoner that the soldiers had to carry him
bodily up the stairs.

Then perhaps at some landing out of reach of the mob,
Paul spoke to the commandant. Of course the Roman
did not know Paul, but he thought that he might be a
certain Jew from Egypt who had led a band of cutthroats
in rebellion against Rome just a short time before. He
was not used to dealing with men like Paul, and when the
missionary spoke so courteously and claimed citizenship
in a prominent Roman city, Lysias let his prisoner speak.

3. Paul's Defense on the Stairs (22:1-21)

The great missionary was still trying to win the unreconciled, whether Jews or Judaizers. So far as he knew
this might be his last opportunity to declare the faith
with boldness. If these people could but hear his own
story, they might recognize his sincerity and the tremendous possibilities of the gospel as he preached it.
Anyway, it was worth the risk.

Men who had just been trying to kill him Paul addressed as "brethren and fathers." The very religion
which they claimed to be defending in manhandling him
Paul now professed proudly. Although he had been born
a Grecian Jew, he had been educated in Jerusalem by the
most highly honored rabbi. He had learned to be just
as zealous for God as they were. Indeed, it was that
zeal for the law which led him to persecute the followers
of "this Way."

But on his way to Damascus the heresy hunter had a
strange and powerful experience. Paul never seemed to
tire of telling that experience. And why should he? He
knew how much it had changed him. Even on the steps
of Antonia he hoped that the story of his conversion
might explain his views. But more that that, he hoped
that the Jewish Christians might see in it the free work

of God's Spirit and learn to love the Gentile Christian brethren.

On this occasion Paul told his story with slight variation from Luke's account in 9:1-9. He described Ananias as "a devout man according to the law," suggesting that though a disciple of Jesus he was still a loyal Jew. Also in this account he told of Ananias' passing on to him his God-given commission.

If the Damascus road experience was to be accepted as genuine and as the work of the Spirit, the commission must be accepted in the same spirit. To underscore that commission, Paul told of his experience in Jerusalem several years later when the Lord had discounted his objection and declared frankly: "Depart; for I will send you far away to the Gentiles" (RSV).

4. Saved from Scourging (22:22-29)

"Gentiles"—that was the word that his audience seemed to have been waiting for. Like the starter's shot to the dash man or the crack of a whip on a horse's back, that word touched off the crowd for immediate action. Like children in a tantrum they screamed, tore off their clothes, and threw dust in the air.

The colonel had had enough! He ordered the soldiers to give Paul the "third degree" to find out what the people had against him. Hustled around by rough soldiers, Paul had no opportunity to speak until the centurion in charge was watching his men make fast his thongs. Then Paul's question sent the centurion scurrying off to find his superior officer. For centuries it had been considered a crime to whip a Roman citizen; certainly the more conscientious judges and officers would not scourge a man when there was no charge against him. Recalling what Roman citizenship had cost him, the colonel may have wondered with scorn how his prisoner managed to get it. Paul's reply was answer enough. His would-be scourgers left him alone.

Although the great missionary was willing to suffer—even to die—for the sake of Christ, he had no martyr complex. He did not seek danger and hardship just to experience them. Only when they were the price of boldly declaring the faith was he willing to endure them. When no principle was involved he had every right to seek exemption from the brutal scourging by asserting his Roman citizenship.

II. To Preserve the Witness (22:30 to 23:35)

Jesus never called on his disciples to take their stand for him and then turn themselves in to the local police. Indeed, he set them an example in avoiding both Roman and Jewish authorities as long as possible. His witnesses were not to be simpletons. As maturing men and women they ought to have sense enough to know when to work under cover and when to take a stand no matter what the consequences. Paul believed that he had dual responsibility: to be a witness and to preserve himself as a witness as long as possible. In the desperate days of his arrest and trials he tried to do both by boldly declaring the faith.

1. Paul Divides the Sanhedrin (22:30 to 23:11)

Paul had to be his own lawyer as he stood before the Sanhedrin, and he chose to begin his defense with a bold assertion. Certainly he did not mean to say that he had been right in everything that he had done. Rather, "he persecuted Christians as a conscientious (though mistaken) Jew (Pharisee) just as he followed his conscience in turning from Judaism to Christianity" (Robertson, 398). But he got no further, for the high priest interrupted with an insulting command. Paul countered it quickly with a strange outburst—strange, that is, when we remember his exhorting other Christians to forbearance and love. But Paul was human, and he may have thought that such an answer was the only kind that would be understood by the overbearing high priest.

Paul's next statement cannot be understood without knowing the tone of his voice in saying it. Of course poor eyesight, which many think was his thorn in the flesh, could have prevented him from knowing who gave the unjust command. Or was the high priest not sitting in his official place or not wearing his official regalia? At least, Paul's prophecy came true, for within about a year Ananias was deposed as high priest and ten years later was murdered because of his Roman loyalties.

Still seeking to preserve himself as a witness, Paul tried a new strategy. Knowing that there were both Sadducees and Pharisees in the Sanhedrin, he identified himself with the latter and claimed that it was on one of their divisive issues that he was being tried. "He implied that the Pharisees, who claimed to believe in a resurrection, should help him, rather than hinder him, in his efforts to convince the Sadducees" (Smith, 186). His whole witness for Christ had been called into question, and the core of that witness was that God had approved Jesus as the Messiah by raising him from the dead. Soon some of the Pharisees began defending Paul, and the two parties got into a hot controversy.

Again Claudius Lysias was frustrated in finding a charge against Paul, and in the midst of the confusion he ordered soldiers to return the prisoner to the castle. Since Paul was a Roman citizen, the Roman officer could not afford to release him to his blood-thirsty accusers without trial.

2. The Jews Plan an Ambush (23:12-22)

As soon as the Sanhedrin saw Paul taken from their midst, they must have realized that they had been tricked. Embarrassed and perhaps wondering what they would do next to get rid of Paul, the leaders of the Sanhedrin were delighted on the very next day to get news about another plot against the prisoner. To get him away from Roman protection he must be requested for another hearing before the Sanhedrin. But of course he would never get there.

Not realizing how much subsequent generations would like to know about the great missionary statesman, Luke very casually introduced a nephew of Paul. The young man heard of the plot against his uncle and reported it to him. Again, instead of being a fatalist, Paul determined to do what he could to preserve himself as a witness. Perhaps because he was a Roman citizen the soldiers were willing to give him some help. Introduced by a centurion, Paul's nephew told his story to Claudius Lysias and urged him not to release Paul to the Sanhedrin.

3. To Caesarea for Safety's Sake (23:23-35)

Jerusalem was one of the trouble spots in the Roman Empire because of the national and religious consciousness of the people. But the Roman colonel probably never thought that the Jews would go to the daring limit of a conspiracy against Roman authority in order to lynch Paul. He had the prisoner in what we would call today protective custody. Having no charge against Paul, he may have been glad to have an excuse to turn him over to the governor. Nearly 500 soldiers were dispatched about nine o'clock that night to take the prisoner to Caesarea along with a letter to Felix the governor.

The words "after this manner" may suggest that Luke gave only the substance of the letter, but it is possible that he heard it read when Paul was brought before Felix. Or a copy may have been given to Paul when he was sent to Rome. The letter itself is a mixture of truth and falsehood. Certainly the colonel did not rescue Paul because he found out that he was a Roman citizen. He would not admit that he had thus far discovered no charge against Paul, nor did he tell how he had prepared to scourge him.

While the conspirators gloated over their hopes for the morrow's ambush, Paul was being escorted away from Jerusalem never to return again. At Antipatris, perhaps halfway to Caesarea, the guard camped for the rest and the night, and only the cavalry went on with Paul to Caesarea on the next day. Felix received him officially, promised to hear his case when his accusers came down, and ordered that he be kept in the palace barracks. Thus far had the Lord preserved Paul as his witness and had encouraged him to be bold in declaring the faith.

III. To SECURE A FAIR HEARING (24:1 to 25:12)

Perhaps the material in this chapter is so distinctively centered in Paul's experiences that general application in these three main subheads is not justified. The idea in the subheads of previous chapters are applicable to modern Christians and churches. For instance, in chapter 4 the modern Christian must be obedient to divine direction through surrender to Christ, adventure in the Spirit, and so on.

Modern Christians must be bold in declaring the faith. As with Paul, that may mean risking our lives to secure for the gospel a fair hearing before the world. That may seem the responsibility only of missionaries in countries positively antagonistic to the gospel. But there's antago-

nism in so-called Christian countries, too.   Ridicule,
disdain, and outright misinterpretation of Jesus by respectable but non-Christian groups furnish Americans
with more opposition than they can now take care of.
We must still be bold in declaring the faith to secure for
it a fair hearing in our own generation.

1. Paul's Trial Before Felix (24:1-22)

Within a few days after Paul's arrival in Caesarea,
Ananias came down with a deputation from Jerusalem,
including a Roman lawyer. When Paul had been called
for trial, Tertullus opened his prosecuting address with
flattering praise for the man who would serve as judge
and jury. Felix had been procurator for about seven
years and had led in dispersing the assassins led by the
Egyptian prophet (21:38). But Tacitus, the Roman historian, claimed that Felix was recalled to Rome two
years later for encouraging bandits in Judea.

With this flattery off his chest, Tertullus stated the
Jewish accusations against Paul: (1) He was a pest, a
common nuisance. (2) He was a revolutionist. (3) He
was a champion of a sect which Tertullus would have had
Felix believe should not be considered as a permitted
religion. (4) He had tried to desecrate the Temple. For
these reasons, so Tertullus claimed, the Jews had arrested
Paul. (V. 7 and some parts of vv. 6 and 8 in the KJV
do not appear in the best manuscripts.)

Then it was time for Paul to give his defense. He,
too, began with a compliment to the governor, but he
avoided flattery. He accepted Felix as his judge and
endeavored to make out a good case before him. Beginning with the last charge of Tertullus, Paul challenged
the Jews to show proof that he had desecrated the Temple, that he had done more than go up to worship. Nor
could they prove that he was an agitator. But he was

perfectly willing to confess his loyalty to "the Way which they call a sect" (ASV). In that loyalty, however, he was only trying to serve the God of the Jews and declare the truth of the resurrection.

To bolster his reply to the accusations of the Jews, Paul began to tell what had happened in the Temple. Then in verse 19 he seems to have changed from defense to offense. No longer did he try to deal with the charges of Tertullus; he began raising questions about those who brought the charges and about the prosecution of the case. Then it was that Felix, who knew more about the Way than the Jews thought, probably realized that according to Roman law the Jews had no case yet against Paul. Thus he postponed the trial until the Roman commandant could come down from Jerusalem.

2. Two Years in Prison (24:23-27)

But Lysias never came to Caesarea, nor was he summoned. Felix had another reason for wanting to postpone the trial. If he saw that the Jews had no case against Paul, he should have released him; but case or no case, that would have offended the very Jewish leaders whom he wanted to get along with. The answer to Paul's continued imprisonment is found in verse 26. That motive is thoroughly consistent with Tacitus' description of Felix: "He reveled in cruelty and lust and wielded the power of the king with the mind of a slave." He had an innocent man in his power and hoped to receive a handsome bribe for releasing him. That must have been the reason he gave Paul so much freedom with his friends in Caesarea. That was the reason he showed so much interest in Paul's message about Christ.

In the sound of that message, however, the Spirit tried to work on Felix. The procurator must have realized at least in part what kind of life he was living, and as Paul discussed the Christian view "of righteousness, and self-control, and the judgment to come" (ASV), that wicked ruler would not let the Spirit lead him from conviction to repentance. Listening with a hardened heart, he was only entertained in subsequent conversations with Paul.

3. Paul Appeals to Caesar (25:1-12)

Those two years in prison must have been a great trial for Paul, who as a missionary had always been on the go, obedient to challenges for broader service, and witnessing actively even when home on furlough. How he and his friends in Caesarea must have hoped that the new procurator might acquit and release the missionary! When Festus visited the religious capital of his region to gain the good will of its Jewish leaders, he found a new high priest on the job; but he and his colleagues were just as bitter about Paul as Ananias had been. Hoping they might trick the new ruler and get rid of Paul without a trial, they suggested that he be brought to Jerusalem for another hearing. Although Festus was not acquainted with Jewish strategy, he couldn't be tricked so easily.

In response to his counter suggestion the Jewish leaders followed him to Caesarea. Perhaps realizing the weakness of their case, they tried to substitute a multitude of charges for their lack of evidence and truth. But even a juryman can recognize that little trick, and Festus was not impressed. Certainly Luke has given us only a summary of Paul's defense, for verse 8 would not be adequate for a trial in which a man had so much at stake. But the summary suggests the charges brought against Paul: heresy, sacrilege, and treason (Smith, 197). On all three counts he gave a flat denial.

Like so many public officers Festus let his judgment be determined by political considerations. He hated to run the risk of getting off to a bad start with the Jews; therefore, he made Paul the very proposition which he had denied when offered by the Jews. Paul the prisoner saw its hidden danger, and as a Roman citizen he asserted his rights. Similar to the way certain cases in our own country can be appealed to the Supreme Court, the Roman citizen had the right to ask that his case be heard by Caesar. Who knows but that as a missionary statesman he saw in his dilemma the opportunity of extending his Christian witness to the Empire's capital!

On the stairs of the tower Paul had been bold in declaring the faith hoping that he might yet win some of the unreconciled. Again in the Sanhedrin his bold stroke was used of the Lord to preserve him as a witness. Now before Festus and the desperate Jewish leaders he was still the bold apostle of the faith when he hazarded all to secure a fair hearing for the gospel.

For Review and Further Study

1. Why did Paul feel compelled to go to Jerusalem?
2. In what two ways did Paul try to win the unreconciled among the Judaizers? How did they respond?
3. Paul believed that God expected him to preserve himself as a witness without betraying his convictions. How did he do it on three different occasions?
4. Why was Paul's case a problem for the Roman authorities?
5. To counter the ridicule, disdain, and outright misinterpretation of Jesus, American Christians must be bold in declaring the faith. Suggest some areas where this must be done.
6. List the various hearings which Paul had as defendant. Why did he make an appeal to Caesar?

IX

FAITHFUL TO THE END

Acts 25:13 to 28:31

I. *One Message for All Men* (25:13 to 26:32)

   1. Festus Invites a King's Counsel (25:13-27)
   2. Paul's Defense Before Agrippa (26:1-23)
   3. The King's Verdict (26:24-32)

II. *Undaunted by Physical Danger* (27:1-44)

   1. From Caesarea to Crete (1-13)
   2. The Storm (14-44)

III. *Facing Life and Death* (28:1-31)

   1. Three Months on Malta (1-10)
   2. Rome at Last (11-16)
   3. Still Preaching and Teaching (17-31)

FAITHFUL TO THE END

Acts 25:13 to 28:31

Of course the book of Acts does not tell of Paul's death, but it closes with him in the city of his martyrdom. For two years he would live under guard. Then before that fateful day of death he probably had several years of freedom and one of bitter and lonely imprisonment. Yet these closing chapters of Acts are typical in many ways of the rest of Paul's life and ministry. Even though we have no New Testament record of his death, in the light of Luke's sketch of his ministry and of reliable tradition we are confident that Paul was faithful to the end of his life.

That phrase does not mean much to those who have lived always in a so-called Christian country. They may know what it means to be faithful throughout a rich and full life without facing any desperate opposition. But most of us do not know what it means to live the Christian life in the face of a government or state church which is determined to eradicate or nullify the witness of evangelical Christians. Every country still under evangelical Christian leadership must be vigilant against the rise of either of these enemies of the Christian witness.

Christians are not asked to seek opposition. They are expected by their Master, however, to make their witness so clear that the Christian point of view may be quite distinct from the world's attitude. In this way the true Christian will inevitably face opposition; and in doing so, he will have Paul's opportunity—to be faithful to the end.

I. One Message for All Men (25:13 to 26:32)

The faithful witness has only one message. Through Bible study, meditation, and experience the Christian's understanding must grow and his devotion deepen. But no matter how keen his insight, no matter how selfless his loyalty, the faithful witness has only one message. Paul summed his up in his first letter to the church at Corinth: "For I determined not to know any thing among you, save Jesus Christ, and him crucified" (2:2).

That one message Paul shared with all men. To Gentiles in Damascus and to Jews in Jerusalem he declared it. To all who would listen in synagogues, market places, and lecture halls he preached the same gospel. A seller of purple in Philippi, a member of Athens' court of the Areopagus, tentmakers from Rome—these and many others needed the same message of salvation. To the rich and poor of many cities, to the apostles and the Sanhedrin Paul had made his message clear. But now in chains he had a chance to preach before a king—to preach his one message for all men!

1. Festus Invites a King's Counsel (25:13-27)

Festus may have been relieved to have Paul appeal to Caesar, but he still had a problem on his hands. Thus far, he had been unable to discover a legitimate charge against the man; yet he could not dismiss the case after Paul's appeal to Caesar. Consequently, the arrival a few days later of Herod Agrippa II must have brought him much relief.

This Agrippa was king of a small territory northeast of the Sea of Galilee. He was part Jew and son of Agrippa I, who had once ruled over most of Palestine and had tried his hand at persecuting the Christians (12:1-3). Acquainted with Jewish history and law, Agrippa feigned some devotion to Judaism, but he was only a puppet of

Rome. With him on this visit of state came his sister Bernice who lived with him as his wife.

To Agrippa the Roman procurator gave a fair statement of the main facts of Paul's case and was frank about his own dilemma, not being able to discover anything in Paul's conduct contrary to Roman law. He was further confused by the reference to "one Jesus, who was dead, whom Paul affirmed to be alive." In reply to Agrippa's polite wish that he might hear the prisoner, Festus promised him the opportunity on the next day.

2. Paul's Defense Before Agrippa (26:1-23)

Some may be tempted to pass over Paul's address, thinking that they already know the facts of his message. But that message had never been declared more eloquently than before Agrippa; this is one of the great addresses of all time. Not only does it make the message plain, but before Paul was through, he was preaching for a verdict.

First, Paul declared his happiness in being privileged to make his defense before Agrippa because he was "especially familiar with all customs and controversies of the Jews" (RSV). Thus far he had found it impossible to defend himself against Jewish charges in a Roman court. Then he claimed that Jews in Jerusalem, if they were willing to testify, could tell the court how loyal he had been to the law in his life as a Pharisee. But now it was because of one of the main teachings of the Jewish faith that he had been accused by Jews. That teaching is revealed in the question Paul directed to the whole assembly: "Why is it thought incredible by any of you that God raises the dead?" (RSV).

As if he saw opposition on their faces, Paul began to tell them the story of his own conversion to show how God's power could change someone just as unbelieving as they. Once, his zeal for the faith of his fathers had led him to persecute followers of Jesus, testifying (as an investigator) against them even when the sentence was death. (This is the probable meaning of verse 10 rather than that Paul was a member of the Sanhedrin.)

But at the height of his career as persecutor a light and a voice had stopped him at noonday near Damascus. Instead of telling of his three days of blindness in the city and of the ministry of Ananias, Paul reported his commission as being given immediately. "We must not overlook that this was a distinct apostolic (missionary) commission. In essential features it is parallel to that of the Twelve and other earlier disciples (Luke 24). It was personal and came to him directly" (Carver, 247). It frankly commissioned Paul to preach to the Gentiles, offering them the same salvation available to believing Jews.

That heavenly vision had become the passion of his life. But it was also the reason that the Jews had wanted to kill him. In spite of opposition, however, he had stood with God's help to proclaim to all men only what the Law and Prophets had envisioned. Then he began to summarize the major doctrines.

3. The King's Verdict (26:24-32)

But Festus had heard enough, and because he didn't understand much of what he heard, he accused Paul of being mentally unbalanced. Even modern respectable Christians take refuge in the same charge when they do not understand the zeal which some others show for Christ and his kingdom.

But Paul knew that Agrippa would understand; at least, the king's knowledge of the Hebrew Scriptures and customs should give him background for making some kind of decision about Jesus of Nazareth and his affect on Paul. Before Agrippa knew what was happening, Paul had turned prosecutor: "King Agrippa, believest thou the prophets?" Then before Paul could challenge him further, Agrippa made a reply whose meaning cannot be accurately understood without knowing the tone of voice and manner with which he spoke. Certainly it does not mean that Agrippa was almost ready to become a Christian. Perhaps the ASV rendering is the best translation: "With but little persuasion thou wouldest fain make me a Christian." Robertson suggests that this probably means: "In (or with) small effort you are trying to persuade me in order to make me a Christian" (453). Yes, that is what Paul wanted, whether it took little or much persuasion.

To Paul's appeal Agrippa gave two verdicts. Of course he realized that Paul had done nothing worthy of punishment and might be set free except for his appeal to Caesar. Perhaps he felt very generous in stating that opinion. But he did not realize that he gave another verdict: He heard the world's greatest missionary of the cross preach the one message for all men, but Agrippa turned his heart away.

II. UNDAUNTED BY PHYSICAL DANGER (27:1-44)

We talk so much about how a Christian ought to handle himself in battling against spiritual evil that we sometimes forget that Christian faith should see us through physical crises, too. Or we adopt the fatalist's point of view and think that resignation is a sign of courage. But there's a great difference between being resigned and reconciled. Perhaps it is because we face so little danger in professing and practicing our faith in Christ that we do not understand the Christian way of meeting danger.

For Paul all life was of a piece, and for the Christian all of it is lived under the watchcare of God. In sickness and in health, in poverty and in wealth the Chris-

tian's life is in the hands of God. Whether coming down
Damascus walls in a basket, stoned and dragged out of
Lystra, or rescued from the blood-thirsty mob in the
Temple, Paul was confident of the Lord's watchcare. The
Christian knows that faith, not danger, is the measure
of a man.

1. From Caesarea to Crete (1-13)

Acts 27 is one of the best pieces of writing in the entire
book, and because of its detail and accuracy, it has been
a bulwark in the defense of Luke as a historian before
the radical critics. It is the best description of ancient
seafaring that we have today. Luke was familiar with
the sea, but he wrote as an educated landsman. He did
not use the technical lingo of a sailor; he "notes what the
seaman would take for granted and omits scientific de-
tails for which he would care most" (Roberston, *Luke
the Historian*, 212). But for these very reasons his account of Paul's voyage has been the more understandable.

Late in August or early in September of A.D. 59 Paul
and some other prisoners were committed to a centurion
for the trip to Rome, a long and dangerous voyage for
that time of year. Since no Rome-bound ship was available, the centurion embarked with his company on a ship
out of Adramyttium, a port near Troas. In some port of
call he expected to transfer his prisoners to another ship
bound for Italy. In a rather small ship driven only by
the wind and piloted without compass or sextant, Paul
and his companions set forth on a 1,700-mile voyage to
Rome.

Either because he was a Roman citizen or because he
was an unconvicted prisoner, the great missionary was
shown unusual consideration by Julius the centurion.
From Sidon they sailed northward with Cyprus on their
left to make use of the winds blowing from the northwest;

for the same reason they had to stay close to the coast of Asia Minor. At Myra the centurion transferred his prisoners and guards to a large grain ship bound from Alexandria to Italy. Still facing a northwest wind, they sailed slowly to the southwestern extremity of Asia Minor and then turned toward Crete, still seeking some land protection against the northwest wind.

They tied up in Fair Havens harbor to await better weather. Sometime after the day of Atonement (October 5, 59) Paul spoke to the officers about the danger of continuing the voyage. He was not prophesying danger, but he was hinting of his respect for the Mediterranean's winter fury. But centurion, captain, and owner (or pilot) decided to try for Phoenix, a better winter harbor about fifty miles westward.

2. The Storm (14-44)

The gentle south wind fooled the seamen. While they were coasting westward, a typhonic wind swept down from Crete's great mountain range (more than 7,000 feet high) and drove them out to sea. The name of the wind was Euraquilo, the northeaster. Not until they gained the protection of the little island of Clauda were they able to haul aboard the skiff they had been towing and reinforce the hull of the ship by tying cables around it. Passed the shelter of Clauda, they began to fear being driven onto the sand banks off North Africa. To prevent that, the captain ordered all sails to be lowered. Thus more than ever at the mercy of the storm, on the next day the crew began to throw some of the cargo overboard. Still desperate to lighten the ship's load, on the third day they discarded the rigging and other furnishings of the ship.

As the storm continued and hope was lost, Paul reminded the hungry men that his previous counsel had been justified. But he spoke in no vindictive spirit; he wanted only to prepare them to receive his heaven-sent encouragement. Soldiers and sailors may have thought it a strange speech for a prisoner. But their courage must have been strengthened to hear a man speak so confidently of the watchcare of his God. Deprived for so long of sun and stars, neither Paul nor his company knew where they were; but the Lord knew, and he would bring them through to safety.

On the fourteenth night after leaving Fair Havens the sailors realized that they were approaching land, and their soundings proved it. But for fear that they might be wrecked on a rocky shore in the darkness, they anchored the ship—and from the stern to keep it pointed toward the land. When the sailors tried to use the skiff to make a selfish try for the land, Paul practically ordered that the little boat be cut away. Paul was trusting in the Lord, but he felt that the Lord would need the sailors to handle the ship safely. Then on the last morning aboard Paul encouraged both passengers and crew and urged them to eat before making the desperate drive upon the beach.

In the early morning light no one recognized the land they were facing, "but they noticed a bay with a beach, on which they planned if possible to bring the ship ashore" (RSV). As they moved toward the land, the passengers suddenly pitched forward as the bow went aground on a shoal built up by two sea currents. When they realized that the ship could not be moved and the surf would beat it to pieces, the soldiers suggested killing the prisoners rather than running the risk of losing them in the sea. But again the centurion showed his interest in Paul and ordered that all make for the land as best they could.

III. Facing Life and Death (28:1-31)

Since we are not telling the whole of Paul's life story and since we feel certain that he was martyred only after a second imprisonment, we think of Paul as not facing immediate possibility of death in this last chapter of Acts as he did several years late. Thus on this first visit to Rome Paul was not facing the distinct alternatives of life or death. But like every Christian in every age he was facing life *and* death!

John recognized how significant was the death of the faithful (Rev. 2:10). But neither he nor any other New Testament writer discounted the significance of the *life* of the faithful. Too many Christians like to think that even in the prime of life they still have time to get ready to be "faithful to the end." Their conceit leads them to push back that "end" into some more convenient future. As a matter of fact, all of us are both living and dying, and "unexpected" death will certainly come to some within the hour of their highest self-confidence in life. Therefore, to be faithful to the end, one must be faithful while facing both life and death. To be faithful in death, one must be faithful in life.

1. Three Months on Malta (1-10)

After the strain and danger of two weeks on the turbulent Mediterranean, the simple hospitality of the natives of Malta was a great comfort to the cold and tired men. Glad to be walking on earth again, Paul began collecting wood for the fire. Then as he laid down one bundle of sticks, the natives gasped. A viper was coiled about his arm! With pagan simplicity they offered a childish explanation. They assumed that the viper had bitten him or would do so; when he showed no ill effects of the encounter, they still revealed their pagan simplicity by suggesting that he was a god.

While Paul and his two companions were guests of the island's ruler, the missionary healed the father of Publius and cured all other islanders who came unto him. Surely he must have been true to his commission and many times told his friends of Him who had saved and empowered him. He had wanted to witness in Rome, and the Lord had promised him that; but on the way he had witnessed on the ship and in Malta.

2. Rome at Last (11-16)

After three months the centurion secured passage for his soldiers and prisoners on another grain ship, which took them in three easy stages to Puteoli. From there their journey would be continued by land. For Paul another great relief came in finding Christian brethren in that port. At their insistence Paul asked Julius, the centurion, for the indulgence of a seven-day visit before going on to Rome, about 130 miles away.

Word of Paul's approach finally reached the Christians in Rome (perhaps while he was resting in Puteoli), and two groups came out from the city to meet him. Paul found the first group at the forum of Appius, forty miles from the capital; a second group greeted him at Three Taverns, ten miles nearer the city. How good it was to have these unknown Christian brethren so concerned for him! They knew of his great desire to visit Rome, and they had longed to have him as a visiting teacher and preacher. But they had never dreamed that he would come as a prisoner seeking justice from the emperor. Whatever their first reaction, Paul led them in demonstrating the Christian spirit: "He thanked God, and took courage."

3. Still Preaching and Teaching (17-31)

In Rome Paul was treated with great consideration. Perhaps Julius commended him to the chief of Roman police. At least, with only one soldier guarding him, he was allowed to receive in his own hired lodging all who might want to visit him.

As in all of his missionary work, Paul established an early contact with the Jews in Rome. He wanted to get personally acquainted with them before they could be prejudiced by some unfair gossip. He wanted to make clear his case: that he had not violated the Jewish faith; that the Romans had discovered no charge against him; that he had come to Rome, not to accuse his nation, but because the Jews had disagreed with the Roman judgment about him. The Jews assured him that they had heard nothing about his case, but they were anxious to know something authoritative about the Way, for it was being spoken against so widely.

That was all the invitation Paul needed to arrange another day when he might declare the gospel to the Jews. A large crowd came for an all-day service in which the missionary used the Law and the Prophets to preach Christ and his kingdom. Surely the missionary was interrupted many times by questions and objections. As usual, the audience was divided. As they were leaving in that frame of mind, Paul recited what may have been a last desperate warning. Because of their heritage of faith in the Scriptures, God's self-revelation in Christ should first be made known to the Jews. But if they chose not to see, not to hear, not to understand, not to turn again, they might as well know that God's salvation had been sent also to the Gentiles.

Again Luke sums up in a few words what must have been an exciting ministry for Paul. So far as we know, the Jews in Jerusalem never sent to Rome any representation against Paul. Without such charges, he was probably freed automatically at the end of two years. But in those two years he kept on doing what he had started out to do: "preaching the kingdom of God, and teaching the things concerning the Lord Jesus Christ" (ASV). With a Roman soldier always at his side or at the door, with no assurance as to the ultimate outcome of his appeal, with a great career of Christian witnessing back of him, Paul proved himself faithful to the end.

There were letters to write to faraway churches. There was a runaway slave to be won to Christ. There were Jews and Gentiles who must hear the gospel. There were young Christians who needed guidance in the faith. With all these things to do, the man who met his Master just outside Damascus and had followed him unquestioningly ever since could never do other than be faithful to the end in teaching and in preaching.

For Review and Further Study

1. Summarize in your own words Paul's one message for all men.
2. What were the main points in Paul's great speech before Festus and Agrippa? How does this account of his conversion differ from those in Acts 9 and 22?
3. What were Agrippa's two verdicts?
4. Trace on a map Paul's journey from Caesarea to Rome, or list six places visited on the journey.
5. What two groups visited Paul in Rome? In what two ways did Paul make his life under guard in Rome a continuation of his ministry?
6. Tell what you know of the closing years of Paul's life.

Jan. 11 - 1949 -
Feb. 1, 1950
Feb. 5, 1950
Feb. 12, 1950
Feb. 15, 1950

2/12

Love #   20
ch.   2.00
Dinner   1.12
Gas =   .50